Lester Morris

"Did You Knows?" of England

NOTABLE, LITTLE-KNOWN FACTS OF BRITISH HISTORY, EXPLANATION AND ORIGINS OF PHRASES, SAYINGS, WORDS, AND NURSERY RHYMES.

with a foreword by

Cactus Pryor

A British Connection Publication

Designed by Lorraine Rylance.

ISBN 0-9662214-3-5

Many thanks to the following friends for their help:

My wife VALERIE, for her encouragement, support, and just for putting up with me! She's not only my wife — but my close friend.

My daughter DIANA, for being who she is. (Yes, she is named for Princess Diana.)

SUSAN LUTON, for courageously taking on the challenge of making my writing palatable. It seems I've discovered an extremely capable editor.

CACTUS PRYOR, for his kind words and for writing the foreword for this book.

My good friend CONNOR VERNON of local TV and radio fame who was the first to read what I wrote and gave me some good advice. (But I didn't leave for England, did I?)

MAGGIE BLISS. GB. A great friend, whose knowledge and wit were very helpful. (And let's not forget her husband, Chuck, for putting up with *her.*)

BEVERLEY KILBY. GB. A great help, as good as Maggie, but much taller. Everyone's taller than Maggie!

PRESTON HAUN, my sixteen-year-old nephew who was my computer saviour. It's amazing what these teenagers know today.

Herb McPhearson and Marshall Davis, both computer whizzes. They certainly know their stuff.

Lorraine Rylance, to whom I give a great big "thank you" because she undertook the task of designing the layout and cover of the book. "Her fingers never leave her hands."

Since I don't find computers particularly friendly myself, these people were of incredible help to me. I have now been trained to not press that HELP button. I just call one of these friends (except Maggie). By the way, if there are any mistakes in this book, blame Maggie. I did.

Contents

Foreword

I am an anglophile. It came with the genes... brought over to America by my great, great, great, great grandfather, Thomas Young. He settled down in Jamestown when it was in the process of becoming America's first housing development. My heritage spoke to me loudly the first time I went to England. There was an incredible sense of *déjàvu,* due in some extent to the number of things *Englandish* that have become part of America. But more than that, listening to the myriad of English accents, walking the cobblestone streets, absorbing the antiquity, experiencing the weather, the personalities, playing the links courses... all this said to me, "I have come home."

My friend Lester Morris has enhanced that feeling of home. He's done it cleverly with this book. I studied British history before going there. I thought I had a pretty good read of the place. Actually, as we say in Texas, I didn't know from nuthin'. I've responded to all of Lester's "Did you knows" with a loud, but joyous uh uh. I also went to the dictionary numerous times to check his vocabulary and/or spelling only to learn that ancient words still correctly live in this book.

"Did You Knows?" of England is juicy with little-known tidbits. They are enhanced with Lester's impish humor. This

makes him one of the most personal guides one could have in the UK. He is your guide on this tour of historic England. And when you next wing over to the old motherland, you will be even more intrigued with the place because of Lester Morris' book.

Lester Morris looks like an Englishman. He should be dressed in ancient costume... perhaps that of a Beefeater. He sounds like an Englishman with a fascinating accent — even more so when delivered in his new home, Austin, Texas. So, never mind the airfare and the hotel reservations. Come along with Lester as he tells you fascinating facts that you did not know.

— *Cactus Pryor*

Introduction

The question I get asked a lot is, "Why did you write another book involving British history when there are thousands of books out there on this very subject?" Good question... well, my answer is this: As far as I'm concerned, you cannot get enough books on British history or any other history, for it is our past with which we mould our future. (I can't remember who wrote that, but it sounds good. I must have read or heard it somewhere — if I didn't, well, I'll take the credit for it.)

Many years ago, while still living in England, I worked in the tour business and ended up as a "Tour Director." Of the many thousands of tourists I had the pleasure of showing my country to over the years, I noticed I could tell which of them had some idea of what I was talking about when it came to the 'nitty gritty bits of English history. The people who didn't know anything about what they were seeing spent most of the time with a large question mark over their heads and had great difficulty absorbing all this historical stuff. Whereas, the passengers with smiles on their faces and some knowledge of the subject took all this information in, nodding their heads in agreement with what I was talking about, finding it a pleasure to actually see the places of interest they had read about or studied before coming over to England.

So you see, touring can be hard work even if you have studied. But it can be very, very hard work if you don't first do a little research about the country you are visiting. This is especially true of Great Britain, where history lurks around every corner and some towns and cities are knee deep in it!

So... the reason I wrote this book (I bet you thought I'd never tell you) is to help tourists or people who have an interest in the old country to learn as much as they can. History is a wonderful subject if you approach it with the right attitude.

This book was written in no specific order. As I thought about a topic that I would normally talk about on tour, I wrote it down. What I would like to do is "whet your taste buds" in the hope that by reading short, interesting bits and pieces, you might just take an interest in the subject of English history, go out and buy some more books or visit your local library. There is a wealth of fascinating history just waiting for you, even if you have no intention of going to the old country. Having absorbed this great subject, if you do travel to Great Britain, you just might end up knowing more than your tour director! (That happened to me once. A passenger was more versed in history than I was! No, it didn't worry me... I just kicked her off my tour. [Just joking, of course.]) Then, you can be on a tour with a smile on your face rather than that big question mark over your head. Enjoy reading this book. It was great fun writing it... you can tell by the number of teeth marks on my computer.

"Did You Knows?" of England

Did you know that Henry VIII had a great passion for beef, as well as for lots of other foods? The story goes that one day, while at Hampton Court, he wandered into the kitchen and saw his cook preparing the day's food. On one table was a pile of meat separate from the rest. "What is this meat?" inquired the King. "This, Your Majesty, is the prime part of the beef and your favourite, called the loin." Henry was rather amused about this and, being in a joyful mood, he apparently withdrew his sword and placed it onto the meat, then ceremoniously said, "I now name you 'Sir Loin.'" And the name has been retained to this day.

Did you know that in medieval days it was common in most houses to scatter straw and thrashings (also spelt "threshings") on the floors? Well, carpets weren't around in those days. To get rid of the smells the really posh people would also throw herbs on the floor, such as basil, balm, cowslips, daisies, sweet fennel, lavender, mint, and violets. Even with all that, it still must have smelt revolting, with the livestock and, of course, the dogs. (Cats were not that popular due to the belief that if you owned a cat you were a witch.) As if all this weren't enough, there were the creepy crawlies that went with the animals. Now to stop the dirty thrashings from moving from one room to another when being constantly walked across, a large plinth, or stone step, was put in each doorway. Even today we refer to an adaptation of this stone as the "thrashold" or "threshold."

Have you heard about Dr. John Hall, the chap who married Bill Shakespeare's daughter Susanna on June 5, 1607? They lived in what is called Hall's Croft, which is situated in the smartest part of Stratford-on-Avon. He was quite an established doctor in that, apart from the local "run of the mill" people (in other words, the commoners), he had patients such as the Earl of Warlock, the Bishop of Worcester, and the Earl and Duchess of Northampton. His fame spread to London and even to the King. His Majesty Charles I offered him a knighthood, yet for some unknown reason Dr Hall refused it. It is generally believed that Bill Shakespeare had his son-in-law in mind when he made a reference to a Lord Kerryman, an aristocratic physician, in the play *Pericles*.

Dr Hall had some very rare remedies for his patients. His entire back garden was full of all sorts of herbs he used in his cures. One of his more famous treatments was a mixture of several herbs with a fine sandy gravel that the patient had to drink quickly. Apparently, this "stuff" (well, what else would you call it?) would flush out the ailing person's stomach and tubes throughout the system, dragging along all the bits and pieces that shouldn't be there. Now, I might have taken that one myself in those days, but I certainly wouldn't touch this next one.

Another of Dr. Hall's famous treatments was for a sore throat. First he would capture a small garden frog and would tie a thin piece of cord or string to the frog's leg. (Are you still with me?) Next, he would ask the patient to open his mouth as wide as he could. Then he would slip the frog into the patient's mouth until the frog refused to go any further. It would simply puff itself up and secrete an enzyme that contained a chemical effective for curing the sore throat... And it really worked! (What I want to know is, who thought of putting a frog in someone's mouth in the first place?) So this is the origin of having "a frog in one's throat."

Did you know that in early medieval days a man could beat his wife with a stick? He was allowed by law to do this. But after a while things got a little bit out of hand, and many people had their own idea of what a stick was — some used one the size of a two-by-four or a four-by-four. Women actually died from their injuries. A law was passed to save lives and to reduce the severity of the injuries by stipulating that a man could only beat his wife with a stick that was the thickness of his thumb. This is where we get the expression "rule of thumb."

What on earth were "bed-steps?" These were steps that helped you to get way up into a four-poster bed. You see, such beds were high off the ground because several mattresses were on them. The bed-steps were shaped like a square box with a padded top and a door on one side, which was called a cupboard. Inside was the famous chamber pot. You used this once you had gone to your privy room, which was the old way of saying private room. Some of the rooms would have more than one chamber pot. Some pots were unique in that they were of gold, silver, pewter, and glazed earthenware. Right up to the late seventeenth century, screens were placed in the corners of dining rooms where the men could go and relieve themselves, while still carrying on a conversation. A good example of this can be seen at Flintham Hall in Nottinghamshire. (In fact, ceramic chamber pots are still in use today in many places in England.)

Did you know that a woman who lived beyond her teen years was considered past her prime to marry? In fact, lots of women were rejected by men, irrespective of their age. Many ended up trying to survive by working in their home from dawn till dusk. The job that was in big demand was spinning, so most unmarried women ended up doing this for a living. Thus, the origin of the term "spinsters."

In the Middle Ages, women let it be known that they weren't married by leaving their hair down. And those who were married simply rolled it up in various fashions to indicate that they were, in fact, spoken for. If a man was looking for a woman, he'd first look at her hair. If it was hanging down then he could go ahead and chat her up. Now, a married woman who wanted a "man on the side" would let her hair down loose to catch one. And thus she was known as a "loose" woman.

Did you know that people in the early days didn't bathe? In fact, some of the peasants sewed their clothes on to wear them for much of the year, only removing them in springtime when it started to get warmer. And even then they wouldn't bathe but rather would strip off all their clothes (not a pretty sight), smear themselves with animal fat, and then take it all off with a flat piece of wood a bit like a scraper. Of course, while doing this they would remove all the dirt, scabs, and lice that had accumulated. After going through all this, you too would have a bright, fresh feeling and look great. Just for a brief moment people might even get to like you. This post-scraping time was when people looked for a mate — hence the term, "a spring bride."

What on earth is a "ha ha-ditch?" Well, you will find these ditches at stately homes, castles, and some manor houses. These incredible ditches were introduced in England around the 1700s by a royal gardener called Charles Bridgeman. This ditch was acutely landscaped with the idea that anyone approaching the premises would not be aware of it. Hopefully, the ditch would cause the intruder to trip or fall down. The residents of the property would then laugh at the intruder's fall, hence the "ha ha" bit. The ditch also acted very similarly to a 'cattle grid' preventing livestock from getting too close to the gardens and dwellings.

Did you know there's a church just off famous Fleet Street in London called St Bride's? It was built in 1700, having been designed by Sir Christopher Wren, who, incidentally, designed and built a total of fifty churches in London. (His masterpiece was St Paul's.) Anyway, it became fashionable to get married at St Bride's because of its name and because of another great feature: the wonderful octagonal layered spire. It also became fashionable to celebrate after the wedding ceremony by having a large wedding cake in the shape of that spire. So this is why we have a "tiered" cake at wedding receptions today. It all relates back to St Bride's in London.

Did you know that in medieval days when a couple was about to be married, monks brewed a drink called mead? The monks gave a bottle of it to the newlyweds as a gift and told them to drink the entire contents during a full lunar month. According to the holy fathers, the liqueur was good for virility and helped to produce fine, healthy children. Remember that the main ingredients of mead are fermented apples in the form of a cider, herbs, spices and — the most important ingredient — honey. This is why we refer to the getaway after a wedding as a "honeymoon." (By the way, you can now sew your clothes back on!)

You're probably familiar with the phrase "bed and board." Why the word "board"? This dates back to medieval days when a hospice owner would put up a sign showing a bed to indicate that a traveller could sleep there. And if the word "board" also appeared on the sign, it meant that food was served as well. The board was a clean surface on one side that, when not in use, might have a vase of flowers placed on it. When it was time to eat, the table top would be flipped over (after the flowers were removed, obviously). Then it served as the eating surface — no doubt full of cut marks and stains from various foods. It is where a guest carved and cut his meat, chopped up any vegetables he had, cut his bread, and no doubt stuck his knife in the table so that it didn't roll away.

The master of the house sat at the end of the table in the only chair that had armrests, called the "carver chair," to carve and distribute the food. What this person was called — the "chairman of the board" — is a term still used today in the business world.

In medieval days, one could apply for a job as a "knocknobbler." I bet you have no idea what this job entailed. (That should give you a clue... the word "entailed.") A knocknobbler was a position for a strong man whose job it was to clear the church of stray dogs. Apparently, dogs used to wander into the church looking for handouts of food, some warmth, or maybe for their masters. You see, in those days the doors to the church were left open during a service so people could come and go. There is a church in Warwick that has old records showing this church did indeed employ a knocknobbler, who was paid the princely sum of two pennies per service.

Did you know that we in England celebrate Guy Fawkes Day on November 5? We light a huge bonfire and set off lots of fireworks to celebrate the failure of Guy Fawkes and company in their attempt to blow up the Houses of Parliament in 1605. (King James I would have been sitting on the throne in the building.)

Not many people know that bonfires go back much further. In fact, during the Stonehenge era an enormous bonfire was lit each year on November 1 to welcome in the winter. (The natives no doubt did it to get warm as well.) That tradition was carried on by the Celtics for years. So when it was decided to celebrate the November 1 job the two traditions were merged.

Remember that Guy Fawkes was the only chap caught trying to light the fuse in the basement of Parliament who wasn't burned when captured. Instead, he was brutally tortured then hung, drawn, and quartered. (That's one way of being in four places at once!) Every year, we put an effigy of Guy Fawkes on top of the bonfire and all have a jolly good time — and maybe a cup of tea.

Talking about fires... did you know that in the early fifteenth century, fires were lit for another special occasion? I've mentioned November 5, but another event of interest was St John's Day, on June 24. The custom was to light three different fires on that day. The explanation, to wit... in the first fire people burned a big pile of exclusively animal bones, having saved them up during the year for this special occasion. (It's a bit like our stacking wood nowadays for cold winter nights.) At midday they would burn a separate large wood fire, maybe just a pile of tree limbs. Then at tea time they would light an enormous mixed wood and bone fire and no doubt stink out the neighbourhood. And — yes, you've guessed it — that's where we get the term "bonfire!" (No doubt they had a cup of tea while they celebrated.)

Did you know that 200 years after the execution of King Charles I, Sir Henry Halford, the royal physician, removed a vertebra from the dead King's remains and had it set in gold? His family used the vertebra as a salt cellar for many years. Later, Queen Victoria, after having used it on several occasions, was told the story of its origin. Well, she was not amused. (When, you might ask, was she amused? Who knows?) She ordered the object to be returned to the royal grave immediately.

While we're on the subject... taking body parts from royal tombs is nothing new. Did you know that William the Conqueror had a hole left in the side of his tomb so that people could touch his royal head? It had to be sealed up because he was disappearing too fast. Even Henry VIII had a finger removed from his body by a laborer working on the royal tomb at Windsor Castle. He apparently had it made into a knife handle. (I bet Henry would have a few words to say about that!)

Have you any idea what a misericord is? You will find these in the great cathedrals of England. They are, in fact, seats found in the choir stalls. The origin of these seats go back to the fourteenth or fifteenth. If you can, imagine standing for long hours during various services that went on for twelve hours! So, what is a misericord? Well, it's a narrow shelf on the underside of a choir seat, on which the priests would discreetly rest their weary bodies. (To put that in English, it means "somethng to perch one's butt on and still look like you're standing." Are you still with me?) Most of themhave unique carvings. Look for them next time you're in one of these magnificent buildings.

Incidentally, "misericord" is also the name of a knife that knights used to carry to end the agony of a wounded man. The Fifty-first Psalm is so-called because of its opening words, "Miserere mei, Deus" (which means, "Have mercy upon me, O God"). And the feasting hall for monks after fasting was called a "misericord."

Did you know that in the Middle Ages a "stock" of wood — or, to use a common term, a "stick" — was used by a royal official to record payments due to the King or Queen? The reason for this was that each time a person made a payment the official cut one notch on one side of the stock (stick) and a second notch on the opposite side. This was done in front of various witnesses. Scribed under each notch was the amount and date of payment. When the final payment was made, a curious act took place. Again in front of witnesses, the stock was ceremoniously split down the middle with a very sharp blade. Then one half, complete with notches, was retained by the exchequer and the other half was given to the person who had just completed the payments. The sticks would then be exchanged so that each party would have equal evidence of the payments. This is where we get the term "stock exchange!"

Did you know that early public executions were an entertaining event? People took their children and refreshments and made a day of it. Vendors set up their booths to sell fruit, bread, and beer. Also for sale was a one-page program of the executions taking place. People would fight to get a good spot, just as we do today. Some folks even spent the night to make sure they had a good view. In some cases, there was a good reason for that. After a person's head was removed, a few characters would jump up and touch the blood or the body. By doing this they believed that as the spirit of the deceased went to heaven it would take all their own illnesses with it, thus relieving them of their maladies. Stories exist of people clutching a body once it had been hung, also hoping to be cured of whatever, even though it might mean hanging on to it all night. (I wonder if the expression "hanging around" comes from this strange act.)

Did you know that around Derbyshire a strange event takes place each year during the spring? The custom of "well-dressing" goes back to about 1350. One of the theories is that those who managed to survive the Black Death decorated the head of the well as an offering of thanks. But others believe that it is an old Roman custom and that decorating the well was to thank the water sprites. When "dressing the wells," a board is placed at the head of the well and designs of all sorts are carefully drawn. Then the whole picture is coloured with petals from all shapes and sizes of flowers and carefully stuck onto the board. It's a pleasure to see them, so if you're in Derbyshire in the spring be sure to look for them.

Did you know that some beheadings didn't always go according to plan? For example, in 1685 the Duke of Monmouth arrived from France with 150 men and gathered support from the counties of Wiltshire, Devon, and Somerset. He then made a half-hearted attempt to overthrow King James II, claiming the latter was a usurper and that he, the Duke, should be King. The King's well-trained army met him at a small town called Bridgewater and defeated the Duke's ragtag army in a mass slaughter. The Duke of Monmouth was of course captured and sent to the Tower of London to await his fate.

Now, the Duke's beheading was a fiasco. To ensure the executioner did a good job, it was customary to gave him a large tip before the event. Yet despite such a tip the axeman made a right pig's ear of the Duke's job, taking not one swipe at his head but five. He obviously got very frustrated. (No, not the Duke.) By now the large crowd was booing and shouting at him, and then they began to throw rotten food. Eventually, some smart aleck at the front passed the executioner up a knife that he used to finally get the head removed. When he held it up the crowd booed him even louder. He started shouting back at them and, now totally embarrassed in front of the audience, threw the head out in their midst so he could make his escape. After that incident the executioner was not allowed to use the blade again (except for shaving).

Keeping to the same story, when the King's men finally got the two pieces of the Duke together, they were going to bury them when some bright spark remembered that the Duke had never had his official portrait painted. So some of the officials promptly got clean clothes on him, cleaned his face, sewed his head back on, stuck him in a chair and — bingo — his portrait was painted. If you don't believe me, next time you're in London you can see that very painting in the Portrait Gallery, which is on St Martin's Street just off Trafalgar Square. (He's the pale-looking chap.)

Guess which King of England Charles Dickens was referring to in this statement: "He was ugly, awkward and shuffling, both in his mind and person. His tongue was much too large for his mouth, his legs were much too weak for his body, and his dull goggle eyes stared and rolled like an idiot's. He was cunning, wasteful, idle, drunken, greedy, dirty, cowardly, a great swearer, and the most conceited man on earth." (I'm not asking *him* for a reference.) The King he was referring to was, of course, King James I, who was also King James VI of Scotland and the son of Mary, Queen of Scots.

Have you ever wondered where the terms "top dog" and "underdog" come from? They actually go back to the days when large tree trunks were cut by hand. If you can imagine one of these tree trunks needing to be cut into planks... what was the procedure? Well, a large pit was dug and the tree trunk laid across the length of the pit. The purpose of this was to have one man down in the pit and one on top with a two-handled saw. You can imagine the chap down below, with all the sawdust dropping on him from each movement of the saw, while the chap on top was in the fresh air and without the sawdust. So, the chap on top was known as the top dog and the one in the pit as the underdog. Such places were quite common where ships were built — places like Buckler's Hard, Hampshire, where, incidentally, Lord Nelson's flagship was built.

Did you know that the early Kings and Queens had a passion for falconry? They had an assortment of birds of prey, whose task it was to increase the royal food supply by catching ducks and other game for the King's or nobles' dinner table. (It is said that Henry VIII used to have as many as eight ducks for supper. No jokes, please.) The chap responsible for carrying the falcons around during the hunt was called a cadger. Suspended from his shoulders was a wooden framework that he carried around him. The birds sat on this framework with hoods on their heads as they waited their turn. (By the way, the trained birds were worth a great deal of money. During the reign of Edward III a person caught stealing a bird of prey was sentenced to death.) From the word "cadger" we get a term connected with the famous sport of golf: "caddie!"

Did you know that in very early Viking times there lived a King called Ethelred the Unready? (This King took so long to get ready that I have to wonder if my wife is related to him.) He was a disaster as a King: he was erratic, cruel, extremely lazy, and always completely unprepared to defend England against invasion by the Danes. In 991 he tried to buy off the Danes rather than fight. When they refused his proposal, he waited until they got on their boats and headed back to Denmark, and then in 1003 he ordered a massacre of all the Danes in the kingdom. This in turn brought on a bloody retribution led by the Danish King. Ethelred, who still wasn't ready, fled to the safety of his relations in Normandy.

In 1005 he got married, and on his wedding night his servants found him in bed with not only his new wife, but with his mother-in-law as well... Now he was ready.

Did you know that in medieval days it was a common sight to see a man walking around a larger town or city wearing an oversized cloak? During summer or winter this cloaked chap not only carried a large wooden bucket, but he also dragged a bundle of dried hay with him. Have you any idea what his occupation was? He was known as a human public convenience. You see, in those days if you wanted to visit a restroom... well, there weren't any around, so you just went anywhere. And if you were of importance you would summon one of these chaps — a bit like hailing a cab. He would come over and wrap the cloak around you while you sat on his bucket and did whatever you had to do. And the straw was for... well, do I really have to tell you? Anyway, you paid him a few pennies for his service, and that was that. (I'm glad that's over.)

Did you know that in the Middle Ages royal banquets used to go on for days? These people were real party animals. During the banquet, members of the court and their special guests were entertained by clowns, jugglers, and fire-eaters. Some musicians played from the minstrel gallery, and others strolled through the crowd. Here's a list of food for about thirty people — a so-called light meal for a banquet at Windsor Castle for Henry VIII: each person was served twenty eggs, three dishes of butter, three loaves of chestnut bread, ten wafers of marzipan, six apples, seven pears, ten oranges, and an average of twenty pints of beer and wine. Then came the main course, which consisted of beef, veal, lamb, pork, game, capons, and — a special delicacy — lark's tongue. (You can see why Henry put on so much weight.)

All the food was served on large, oval-shaped loaves of bread called trenches. The bread had to be about four days old to be hard enough to withstand the onslaught. The King and his nobles would go through four and sometimes eight of these trenches during a meal. The other guests had to share not only trenches but drinking vessels as well. They used a knife to cut food and ate with their fingers. (Forks didn't become an every-day eating tool until the Crusaders brought them to England.)

The nobles always carried their own knives and forks and drinking vessel, because in those days it was considered a status symbol to be seen carrying these items on one's person. Then if they were invited to dine, they could do so in the manner in which they were accustomed.

While we're on the subject of food... did you know that in the early castles a certain member of the chaplain's department was called an almoner? His job was to make sure all the leftover food was collected. After the staff was fed, he would distribute the scraps to the poor at the back of the castle. These unfortunates were especially fond of the trenches, as they were usually still swimming with morsels of food and lots of tasty juices. The poor, it has been said, used to fight over such delicacies.

The almoner's job also consisted of visiting lepers, prisoners, widows, the sick and poor, and any other soul in want, including visiting wanderers who constantly roamed the country. He would also collect discarded horses, clothing, and anything else that could be used by those in need.

Did you know that England's early roads were created by the Romans? (Let's face it — they were in England for over 400 years so, having those big fancy chariots as they did, they had to come up with something.) A network of roads, all centred in London and totalling some 5,000 miles, ran throughout the country. This was a tremendous achievement for those chaps from Italy in the funny costumes. The roads were very straight, and travel on them was quite fast. Near the Scottish border you can still see some fine examples of ridged Roman roads, their ridges having been formed from constant use. The most famous of these roads were the Ermine, the Foss Way, and, the longest of them, Watling Street, which started in Dover, went right through London, and ended up in Chester. The roads and their names are still used today.

When the Romans left England, the roads fell into disrepair. Many of them had been grown over to such a degree that to restore them would have been too costly. There was, in fact, no system of repair until the sixteenth century, when the local parishes were made responsible for the roads and their maintenance. Toll roads were introduced to pay for the service and construction of additional roads. A similar system was adopted in Scotland in 1669. Then in 1726 General George Wade was given the first modern government-sponsored road construction project: to build a network of roads throughout Britain. In Scotland he built most of the major highways with foundation stone he took from Hadrian's Wall. This famous structure had been built by Emperor Hadrian from about 122 to 127 A.D. Its original length was seventy-three miles long and ten feet thick — in some places twenty feet thick — and roughly twelve feet high. But that's another story.

Talking about stones... did you know that the Scottish Kings used to sit upon a stone when they were crowned King of Scotland and that this stone was known both as the stone of Scone (pronounced *skoon*) and the stone of Destiny? Several stories are connected with it. One myth is that the stone was used as a pillow by Jacob when he dreamed of "Jacob's ladder," as related in the Book of Genesis. The story continues that Jacob's sons supposedly carried the stone to Egypt. From there it went to

Spain, then all the way to Ireland, where it was placed on the sacred hill called Tar. When an Irish King was seated on the stone at his coronation, it was supposed to groan aloud if the claimant was royal and remain silent if he was a pretender. (This could be the original blarney stone.) From Ireland the stone made its way to the island of Ion in Scotland.

Now this is where King Edward I makes his appearance. His ambition was to conquer Scotland. He even gave the instruction that when he died, if he or his sons had achieved his goal then his bones had to be carried at the head of the army and buried in Scotland. This was not to be, as Scotland has never been conquered. But in 1296 on one of his raids he went to the palace of Scone near Perth and took this sacred stone back to London. He had his carpenter, called Walter the Painter, build him an impressive chair to house this sacred stone. Every King and Queen who has ever been crowned at Westminster Abbey has sat in that very chair complete with stone. (You can see the chair when you visit.)

Yet the former Prime Minister, John Major, claimed that it should be returned to Scotland, from where it was stolen. Well, we've had it 700 years, and I don't know if it has given the royalty of England any luck. Who knows? It might do them some good to take it back. Incidentally, the stone was stolen by four young Scottish nationalists, but was returned just in time for the coronation of our present Queen, Elizabeth II, in 1953... And the story of the stone of Scone will undoubtedly continue.

By the way, the idea of sitting on a stone to be crowned King goes way back in English history. The early English Kings sat on a stone for their coronation, and this all happened at a place that still bears the name — which few people know — of Kingstone-upon-Thames.

Did you know that a tragic infectious disease caused by flea-ridden rats was carried by boat from Siberia and invaded England around 1348? This early incident of the bubonic plague was better known as the Black Death. The reason for that name was... well, it literally turned the victim black and then he or she died. This was during the reign of one of our great Kings, Edward III, and it brought about a dramatic change in history. The country couldn't defend itself, particularly against the French, so most of what had been captured in conquest was lost. Half the population of England was also lost.

In 1665, during the reign of Charles II, the disease made another appearance. The Great Plague of London started in a house around Drury Lane in December of 1664, although records show that a few bizarre deaths had been reported here and there prior to this. As the spring brought warmer weather, more deaths were reported; and it was soon officially pronounced to be the bubonic plague. Unfortunately, the weather became unseasonably hot that year, causing the disease to spread rapidly. As a result, panic set in. People were fleeing (no, not fleaing). They gathered whatever they could take and escaped, in some cases taking the plague with them. By September of 1665, it was recorded that in one week alone 7,165 people had died of this terrible disease in central London. The economy of the country was at an all-time low.

Did you also know that the symptoms of the bubonic plague were large blistery red rings that appeared all over the body? No one had any idea how to treat the victims. It was common for people to carry posies of herbs in their pockets, around their necks — anywhere they could put them. The posies were also placed around windows and doors and in the fireplace. Obviously, people selling herbs made some good money — as did the so-called doctors called "quacks." They acquired this name because of their appearance: their torso was covered with a full-length leather coat, their hands with gauntlet gloves, their eyes with a pair of goggles, and their nose with a large cone. (Just like an ice cream cone.) The cone was filled with herbs of all sorts and fastened onto the nose by a strap around the head. (I suppose you could call it a "potpourri cone.")

Following the red rings, the next major symptom was violent sneezing. Now when this began, death was inevitable, so the victim would look for a priest to be given his last rights. Well, you might know where most of them — along with the doctors — went to save themselves. They had moved well away from London to the countryside. So frequently there was no one who could administer to the dying person. In many cases a close relative or friend would do the honours.

Because of this tragic bit of history, even today we respond to someone's sneeze with "bless you." And we hear children making a reference to the bubonic plague as they recite:

"Ring a ring of roses, a pocket full of posies,
A tissue, a tissue, we all fall down... dead."

This is the original English version. The last word was removed centuries ago, apparently for being not quite appropriate for a nursery rhyme.

Did you know that Queen Elizabeth II, when she was in her school days, didn't like the idea of having another long day of learning French, so she decided to tip an entire bottle of ink over her head? This got her tutor's attention and she got her way, as it took the rest of the day to remove the ink stain out of her hair and skin. (And we wonder where Charles gets it all from.)

Have you heard of a prince called Bladud? (I wonder how he got a name like that.) Now the story goes that this prince, son of King Lud Hudibras, was stricken with leprosy. And such was everyone's horror that he was kicked out of the royal court and banished from the kingdom. Well, after a period of wandering, the only job he could get was that of swine herder. But it didn't take long before all the pigs were infected with the disease. He was sick as a parrot when he saw this, knowing that he might lose the animals.

Then something strange happened. He came across a large area of hot, bubbly, muddy water. Well, it didn't take long for the pigs to start rolling around in all this stuff — they thought the place was hog heaven. After spending several days there the prince noticed that wherever the mud had dried on the pigs, their skin was not only clean but free from the disease. "Could it be the muddy water that had cured them?" he thought to himself. Without hesitating he stripped off his clothes and wallowed in the mud with the creatures. Well, no doubt you're ahead of me. He ended up fit as a fiddle. He was soon running back to his kingdom (once he'd put his clothes back on), and after a thorough examination he was welcomed back into the court. He vowed that when he became King he would build a town by the muddy hot springs. Thus, the famous city of Bath was born.

Did you know that the English game of cricket was declared illegal by Edward IV in 1477? He thought it was an idle, lazy, silly game and that people should make better use of their spare time. Anyway, somewhere down the line the citizenry began to ignore this law (as they did many other unnecessary laws in those days) because cricket was soon back in full swing.

Yet if this law had still been in effect in 1715, it would have prevented a dramatic change in the royal succession. You see, George II's eldest son, Prince Fred, had a great passion for cricket and was responsible for its popularity in the south of England. Well, one day during a match, the batsman hit the ball (roughly the size of a baseball and much harder) that struck the Prince a mortal blow on his chest. Yet King George was unmoved by the death of his son. The funeral service was held at Westminster Abbey, but the King ordered that there should be no bishops or peers, nor could anthems be sung. No food was provided for the mourners; they had to go to the nearest bar. The public didn't like the royal family, but they liked Fred. He was, if you will, "one of the lads." So after his untimely death, the following poem, which is self-explanatory, became popular:

> "Here lies Fred, who was alive and is dead.
> Had it been his father, I had much rather.
> Had it been his brother, still better than another.
> Had it been his sister, no one would have missed her.
> Had it been the whole generation, still better for the nation.
> But since 'tis only Fred, who was alive and now is dead,
> There's no more to be said."

Now, most people are very confused with how the simple game of cricket is played. So to make it very easy, these are the (simple) rules. In the game of cricket there are two sides, one out in the field, one in out of the field. (Are you still with me?) Each man on the side that's in goes out, and when he's out, he comes in, and the next man goes in until he's out. Now, when they're all out, the side that's been out in the field goes in, and the side that has been in out of the field goes out, and they try to out those coming in. (Easy, isn't it!) Now, if the side that's in declares, then you get men still in — not out — then, when both sides have been in... and out... including not out twice, then that's the end of the game. (I bet you feel much better about cricket after reading this.)

Did you know that in 1283 King Edward I, who was known in history as Longshanks because of his long legs, finally conquered Wales and killed the Welsh prince Llywelyn? Naturally, the Welsh people rebelled and complained to Edward that he'd killed their prince. Well, Edward cried out to the crowd that he would be their leader. But the Welsh people were sick as a parrot upon hearing that. So they shouted back to Edward, "We don't want an Englishman! We want someone born in Wales — and who doesn't speak English!" Without hesitation, Edward went into his castle and within minutes returned with his newborn son, put him in his upturned shield, held him above his head, and shouted to the Welsh crowd, "I give you my son. He was born here in Caernarfon Castle [in Wales]. And he does not speak English." Both parties in the conflict seemed to come to a sort of agreement, and this is why the eldest son of every King or Queen since 1284 has been awarded the title of Prince of Wales.

By the way, by law the prince must learn to speak the Welsh language (which, from my experience, you have to learn to spit a lot when speaking it).

While we're on the subject of Edward I, who was one of England's great warrior Kings... did you know that he married a beautiful woman named Eleanor of Castile in 1254? (It was on a Wednesday and it was raining.) Well, he loved her so dearly that he took her along on a Crusade from 1270 to 1273. After they returned home to England, they began touring and sorting out the odd uprising here and there around the country. At one point a man attacked Edward, stabbing him in the arm with a poisoned dagger. Here's a poem written during that period.

Edward I was strong and tall.
He had the longest legs of all.
And when from one who wished him harm
A poisoned dagger pierced his arm,
Edward was weak as other men.
His long legs could not help him then.
So Eleanor, his gentle wife,
Sucked out his wound and saved his life.
And when in time his lady died,
All through England far and wide,
He built stone crosses to be seen
In memory of the Longshanks' Queen.

Edward was devastated that his wife had died without notice. He is said to have cried out these words: "My heart is turned to mourning. In life I loved her dearly, nor can I cease to love her in death." She had died at Hadby in Nottinghamshire, so he had to travel to London with her body. Now, wherever he and his retinue rested overnight, Edward ordered a cross to be erected in her memory. These crosses are known as the Eleanor crosses. The overnight stops were at Lincoln, Grantham, Stamford, Geddington, Northampton, Stony Stratford, Woburn,

Dunstable, St Alban's, Waltham, and the two in London, West Cheap and Charing Cross. (The latter, the most famous of them all, isn't the original. That was destroyed by the Puritans, and later a replica was placed outside the Charing Cross railway station.) Out of the twelve that were erected, sadly only the four at Geddington, Northampton, Waltham, and West Cheap remain.

Did you know that Henry V (you know the one whose hair-dresser stuttered with his hands? — a very rare haircut for those days) got sick as a parrot one day when he received a large number of tennis balls from the King of France, Charles VI? (They were very hard balls in those days.) The balls were accompanied by a note telling him that "you would be better off playing tennis than trying to make war with France." Well, talk about an invitation. Apparently, Henry kicked up a racquet. (No puns, please.) He went to France complete with the balls (the tennis ones) and had a tremendous victory at the Battle of Agincourt (which we all know about, so we won't go into that)... And what happened to the tennis balls? Please don't ask.

Did you know that at one point England, as part of its defence, had one of the most powerful weapons in existence? This was the crossbow, and it came in all shapes and sizes — even some that could fire two bolts at once. The idea had apparently originated with the ballista, a huge machine capable of destroying large sections of castles. The lethal crossbow was actually forbidden by the Church. But King Richard I was an expert shot with the thing, and he encouraged its use. Yet the irony is that a bolt fired by a crossbow killed him while out hunting. The Church claimed it was God's will that he should have been killed in such a manner.

The bolts, or arrows, used for the crossbow were of various sizes. The heads on them varied in size and in shape as well, according to the intended subject. These heads were called quarrels, and this is where we get the saying "to pick a quarrel."

You probably know that England's patron saint is called St George. Yet few people know that throughout its history saints abounded there. In fact, there was just about one for each day, and they were responsible for all sorts of things. For example, if you were a beekeeper your saint was St Ambrose, and your neighbour the farmworker's saint would be St Walstan. If you lost something St Anthony was there to help you find it. If you suffered from leprosy you would turn to St Giles. Even if you had a headache St Stephen would give you comfort.

Did you also know that in the eleventh century there were over fifty shrines to saints in England? St Albania's shrine was the first to be constructed, followed by St Gregory's, the apostle of England. Two Kings of England also ended up as saints: Edward the Confessor and the King of East Anglia, King Edmund, who was martyred in 869. But why on earth, considering the great number of saints that could have been adopted, did England end up with St George as its patron saint when he never even set foot in the country?

We go back to Richard I, known as Richard the Lion Heart, who was King of England. When Richard was on his Crusade in the Middle East, he apparently placed his army under the protection of St George while attacking the city of Antioch in 1098. Well, Richard told his famous version of the story of the knight in shining armour: how George rescued a beautiful princess by slaying the dragon that was about to attack her.

This legendary story has been told, retold, and elaborated upon by many storytellers and scholars — so much so that even when the great King Edward III came along, he fell in love with this sort of stuff, especially the legends of King Arthur. Edward became so enthralled that he even instituted the Most Noble Order of the Garter, the highest order of knighthood in England, and he inducted forty of his most trusted knights into the Order in St George's name. It was Edward who built St George's Chapel in Windsor Castle. And because of these acts he proclaimed George as the saint of soldiers. Thus, the country adopted this saint as its patron saint.

Remember the famous words of Henry V when he cried out at the Battle of Agincourt in 1415: "the game's afoot, follow your spirit; and, open this charge, cry God for Harry, England, and St George!" So it wasn't until 1450 that St George was officially recognized.

By the way, Edward III's great ceremony, the Order of the Garter, can still be witnessed each year at Windsor Castle on June 15. (You can obtain tickets to watch the event by contacting the Windsor Tourist Information Centre.)

Did you know that thousands of tourists at one time or another have watched the famous changing of the guard at Buckingham Palace? If you haven't seen this event then you're in for a treat. Now, these chaps not only guard Buckingham Palace but also St James' Palace, Windsor Castle, and the Tower of London. And they perform the famous ceremony of the keys each night at ten o'clock as well. Did you know they also used to be on guard inside the Bank of England? But what with sophisticated security they were kicked out in 1973.

Most people like to watch the trooping of the colours that celebrates the Queen's official birthday and the state opening of Parliament. These are in addition to the daily event (daily except during the winter months, when it takes place on alternate days). Now, the bright red uniforms are the guards' distinctive trademark. Yet not many people know that the first ceremony of foot soldiers goes back to the Grenadier Guards, formed in 1656. These were the chaps who won that great victory at the Battle of Waterloo. In fact, this is where they stole those big bearskin hats — as a victory prize at this very battle. Then there are the Scots Guards. These chaps originated with Charles I in 1642, but returned to England in 1685. The Coldstream Guards were formed by a General Monk in 1659, their name coming from the general's home village of Coldstream on the Scottish border. The Irish Guards (yes, they actually came from Ireland) were a fairly recent addition, originating in 1900. And, last but not least, the Welsh Guards came fifteen years later, in 1915.

Now, many people say to me, "They all look the same. How on earth do you know who's who?" Well, it's easy when you know what to look for. There are two major differences. First look at the collar: each side has the symbol of that regiment — the Scots have a thistle, the Grenadiers a grenade, and so on. But the main thing to look for is the set of buttons down the front of the tunic, or jacket. The buttons are sewn on differently for each regiment. The Grenadiers have buttons in a more or less normal arrangement of one line. The Coldstream Guards have theirs in pairs, two then space then two, and so forth. The Scots Guards' buttons are placed in threes, the Irish Guards' in fours, and the Welsh Guards' in fives. So the next time you're in London you'll be able to identify who's who among these chaps.

Did you know there's a famous street in London off Whitehall that was built in the mid-seventeenth century? It was purchased by the Crown during the reign of George II. The street was built by Sir George Downing. (He was, incidentally, the second graduate of Harvard College, during the time his family were residents of America.) George had a favourite minister named Sir Robert Wallpole, whom he wanted living closer to Parliament. So he purchased the street and gave it to his right-hand man, now titled Prime Minister, who took up residence there. It has since been the permanent residence of all prime ministers. Sadly enough, you can't go down there as you could in the old days. For security reasons there's a very large gate across the road to stop the public from entering.

Did you know that in London there's a place called Speaker's Corner at the end of Hyde Park near Marble Arch? (Incidentally, Marble Arch was designed by the famous architect John Nash in 1828. It was the main entrance into Buckingham Palace. But the "not amused Queen" Victoria, who was the first monarch to live at "Buck" Palace, said she didn't like it because it scared the horses pulling her carriage. (It never occurred to her that it could have been her they were scared of.)

Well, back to Hyde Park. It used to be the hunting ground of Henry VIII and was known as Manor Hyde. In the corner of this famous park is Speaker's Corner, where people have gathered for over 600 years. In 1872 this site was granted a legal bill of assembly, which simply means that you get on your soapbox and talk on any subject you like, whatever your creed, colour, or persuasion, as long as you don't say anything that's blasphemous or incite a breach of the peace.

Did you know that in 1634 King Charles I, who was desperate for money to gather troops, imposed a "ship money" tax? The fact that he was scraping the bottom of his financial barrel motivated him to discover an old decree by which "ship money" was levied from maritime towns and villages. This tax was also used to build up naval funds. In other words, people living on the coast would be expected to pay the tax. But desperate as Charles was for money, he changed the law in 1640 and made the entire citizenry pay this outdated tax. The people naturally rebelled. Records show that one John Hampden refused to pay. In a test case the judges pronounced in favour of the King, and Hampden was subsequently thrown into prison and never seen again. So Parliament had to step in and declare the "ship money" tax illegal in 1641. Poor King Charles was sick as a parrot, and eventually he was forced to find other methods of raising revenues.

While we're on the subject of King Charles I... he couldn't get into London during the Civil War because Parliament was controlling it. So to get around his money problem, which made him desperate, he did it this way. He asked all his supporters to donate their silver or gold objects to him in order to save his troops. Then he melted down the objects to make token money to pay his troops with. You see, his troops weren't getting paid, and they had started making hints like "But Cromwell's troops get paid well." Some, in fact, moved from the Royalists to the Roundheads.

Some of the buildings in which King Charles minted coins still exist today, including a pub in Southam, Warwickshire, called, logically, The Old Mint.

Did you know that a Welsh man called Richard Trevithick designed the world's first railway locomotive? It ran at Pen-y-darren, located in South Wales, on February 21, 1804. But in 1829 along came the modern steam engine. It was named the Rocket and was designed by Robert Stephenson and Harry Booth. These men won the Liverpool and Manchester railway locomotive trials.

And did you know that on September 15, 1830, when all the dignitaries boarded the train for its first run with passengers, the pessimists were there? (Yes, they were around even in those days.) Trying to discourage the dignitaries from taking this fatal journey, they handed out information sheets full of reasons why no one should travel on this evil monstrosity. The message they were trying to put over was that when the train reached its maximum speed, the passengers' "lungs would collapse." Well, the top speed in those days was... are you ready for this?... seven miles per hour. You can see the Rocket at the railway museum in the great city of York. (Incidentally, this is where the first railway station was built in England, which is why the city was selected for the museum.)

By the way, did you know that the gauge of railway tracks was started in England those many years ago and that the rest of the world uses the same measurements: 4 feet 8-1/2 inches?

Did you know that the "spinning jenny" was a machine patented in 1770 by a man named John Hargreaves? His invention could spin a number of threads simultaneously. What it accomplished was to extend the principle of the spinning wheel by carrying many spindles (about 120) vertically. He'd gotten the idea for it when his daughter knocked over a spinning wheel on its side. His invention was a great success and was used until the nineteenth century. (By the way, his daughter's name was Jenny — hence, "spinning jenny.")

Did you know that in the eleventh century a royal official replaced the earl as the King's chief agent in a shire (the equivalent of a county)? What this meant was that he was responsible for collecting the royal taxes. The official's title, "reeve shire," stuck for many years. But later it was corrupted and turned around, and the official became known as the "shire reeve." Even further on in history the name got changed to "sheriff," which we still use today, but not in the same capacity as in America. The sheriff's job in England is chiefly to supervise Parliamentary elections, execute writs, and summon jurors. (So if your last name happens to be Reeve, now you know where your name originated.)

Did you know that when William I conquered England in 1066, one of the first things he did to stabilize the country was to have a survey taken of all its inhabitants? He sent his troops out with some of his officials with instructions to record everything in the land. (When you think about this, it took a very clever man to come up with such an idea; nobody before him had even thought about it — let alone do it.) His men checked and double-checked all the people of the land, all the livestock, all the houses, churches, and farms, all the machinery — in short, anything that could be recorded was written down. When they'd finished, William sent them out again to triple-check.

After some twenty-odd years this mammoth book was completed. The people of England called it the Domesday Book because once something was written in it an individual was "doomed" — there was no chance for appeal. Now, the entire reason for this great book was to be able to lay out a tax system so that William could run this country that he'd stolen. The reason that William conquered England was that the kingdom had been promised to him by his great-uncle Edward the Confessor, who had "popped his clogs" (died, that is). So the entire basis of our present tax system goes right back to the Domesday Book, which was finally put together in 1086. It can still be seen at the public records office in London.

Did you know that William I, known as the Conqueror, had three sons named William, Henry, and Robert? Apparently, William thought that Robert, the oldest, wasn't capable of running the country, so he bequeathed the kingdom of England to William, who became William II. Robert was given the dukedom of Normandy; and to the youngest, Henry, he left a large sum of money. William Rufus, as William II came to be known because of his bright red hair and ruddy complexion, feared God little and man not at all, practised every known vice, swore continuously, and had a vile temper.

Well, the story goes that one day — August 2, 1100, to be precise — William Rufus was out hunting in the New Forest, which is a large forest near Southampton in Hampshire. The King was charging around with his entourage when an arrow coming out of the blue hit him right in his heart. The historians, who were monks and couldn't stand him, recorded it thus: "an arrow slighted off a tree and struck the King a mortal blow." Sir

Walter Tyrel, a member of the hunt, put spurs to his horse, headed for the coast, and disappeared somewhere in France, never to be seen again. The reason for his flight was that he and the King had quarreled fiercely the night before, and he didn't want people to think he was responsible for the arrow, as no doubt they would have. But guess who else was in the hunting party? The King's younger brother Henry, who also put spurs to his horse, but not to go to the coast. Instead, he went directly to Winchester, the capital of England at the time. Henry claimed the fortune and the gold hat and wasted no time in being crowned King of England. As for William Rufus, well, his body was stripped, thrown into a horse-drawn cart, and taken to Winchester Cathedral. The monks didn't want to bury such a wicked man on hallowed ground, but they had no choice. One year later the tower of the cathedral collapsed, and the monks claimed that it was God's doing for their having buried such an evil man on consecrated soil. When visiting Winchester Cathedral, you can see William Rufus' tomb. And in the New Forest there is a marker showing the spot where he was killed.

Did you know that England had several famous pirates? There was one in particular who was known as Blackbeard, although his real name was Edward Teach. He apparently feared nothing and most people feared him, and that suited him fine. He was, if you like, a disgusting, filthy, swearing drunk who never washed his clothes. His coat and trousers had permanent stains from a variety of different-flavoured foods, blood, and drinks. His favourite drink was rum, which he consumed quite often. When he wanted to impress people he would add a drop of gunpowder to the liquor and, just before drinking, would light it. Now, I thought I knew some party animals.

Talking about drink... did you know that beer in the early days was not as strong as it is today? Yet to a child it was still quite potent. Well, it's on record that during 1632 beer was prescribed to children of all ages. In fact, a quantity of two and a half gallons was added to their weekly rations. I wonder if the parents sung them nursery rhymes or told them jokes.

Did you know that in medieval times the monks were fairly clean people compared with the rest of the population? Way back in those days there were washrooms in the monasteries and, of course, the nunneries as well. It's recorded that three or four times a year the monks and nuns had hot water for bathing, whether they needed it or not. And while they had the hot water they took advantage of it to wash their hair (or, at least those whose heads hadn't been shaved). No shampoo — they had to make their own by mixing ashes from different woods, a variety of herbs, and water. Now you can see why they wore those hoods.

While we're on the subject of hair... did you know that it was a common sight to see lice and creepy crawlies on people? Rich or poor, the bugs didn't care. Most people had their own ideas of how to rid themselves of these pests. No, they didn't have bug spray in those days. So how did they get rid of them? Well, they simply picked the nits off themselves, or got a relative or friend to pick them off just like you see monkeys do it. Fleas and lice caused the death of many newborn children since most of the bugs carried some form of disease. (Makes you want to start scratching, doesn't it?)

Did you know that Elizabeth I used sulphur powder on her face, which is, of course, an acid? Now, this substance will actually kill off red corpuscles and in turn make your face white. During the Elizabethan period it was fashionable to look like you'd just seen a ghost! The white complexion was supposed to be a beautiful sight. Well, to some people it might have been, but it was slowly eating away Elizabeth's skin. She must have looked a rare sight indeed since she had hardly any hair at the back of her head. (Incidentally, after her death eighty wigs, all ginger-colored, were found in her changing room.) Her teeth were black as the ace of spades, so undoubtedly her breath must have been... well, you know. You see, she loved chocolate, a treat introduced to her by Sir Walter Raleigh. She's said to have liked it very hot, very sweet, and very often.

So, all things considered, Elizabeth wasn't that good-looking. I have a feeling this is why she wore all those pearl necklaces, big jewels, and fancy-coloured dresses. That way, her spectators would be too busy looking at all the stuff hanging on her to look at her face. Yet, having said all that, she was a brilliant Queen of England. And a virgin Queen at that.

By the way, apparently she did make an effort to clean her teeth. The toothpaste of the time was a mixture of honey, crushed bones, fruit peels, a variety of herbs, and soot from the chimney. If the teeth were stained, crushed pumice stone, alabaster, or even crushed brick would be added. This compound would be rubbed on the teeth with a cloth or fingers. When Elizabeth died on March 24, 1603 (it was Wednesday and it was raining), after having reigned for 44 years and 127 days, she hardly had a tooth in her mouth. So we all know how miserable she must have been.

Did you know that from the very early days right up to the nineteenth century, if you committed suicide it was considered a crime and, furthermore, that criminals, irrespective of their crime, could not be buried on consecrated ground? So where were they buried? Well, the next closest thing to a Christian burial was to be laid to rest at one of the major crossroads. This was due to the cross formed by the intersection of the two roads. The road was simply dug up, then the suicide victim's body was popped down in the hole and covered over. So when you drive over the crossroads of England, you may well be driving over someone's grave.

By the way, whenever paved roads were being constructed over the dirt ones, if workers discovered a body they would simply bury it on the side of the road.

Did you know that during the early days of public hangings a chap named Roger Hammond was hanged in 1707 for a murder that he never confessed to having committed?

Well, the story goes that on the day in question he was picked up in a horse-and-cart and taken to the hanging place, called a tyburn. He and the witnesses were heading out of town to the place of execution. But just before they left town they stopped at a pub. The witnesses asked Hammond if he would like a drink on the house before the job was to be done, and he refused — the fool. He claimed he just wanted to get on with it, so they continued. (Not many people know that if someone was to be hung it was customary to buy him some drinks to get him roaring drunk. Then, when he was on the gallows, he wouldn't give a hoot as to what was happening. Some people were hung singing pub songs — no, not the hanging tree song.) Returning to the story... they got Hammond all strung up, and the deed was over in no time. Well, the lads wanted to get back to the pub and drink his beer. But what happened was that soon after Hammond was pronounced dead, the King's messenger rode up with a reprieve and ordered that his execution be stopped.

There has to be a moral here somewhere. Perhaps: if someone offers you a drink, take it! Especially back in those days, it could have saved your life.

Have you ever thought about why we count 1-2-3 before we do something? Why don't we count 1-2-3-4 or 1-2-3-4-5? Why is it always 1-2-3? Well, this goes back to crime and punishment in medieval days. You see, a person who had committed an offence might be tried for it with the following procedure: A large cooking pot called a cauldron was hung over a fire. The amount of water that was put in to boil was determined by how severe the crime had been. It might be three or four inches, or half full, or go right up to the top of the pot. Once the water was boiling a large rock was dropped in. The suspected criminal had to put his hand into the water and pick up the rock, keeping his hand submerged through the count of 1-2-3. Then the authorities would bandage his hand and send him home. In 1-2-3 days' time the potential criminal had to go back to have the bandages taken off. If the wound had blisters on it, the person was guilty and was put in the stocks or in prison for — guess what? — 1-2-3 days. So this is where the custom comes from. Come hell or high water.

Did you know that the Roman Emperor Julius Caesar was the chap who gave us the Julian calendar? (Obviously, it was named after him.) Unfortunately, it was discovered that the calendar was losing eleven minutes a year. So by 1582 the world was ten days in front of itself. To solve the problem Pope Gregory ordered that the ten days be dropped from that year. All the countries did... except England. The country refused to do such a thing and stood defiant on the subject until 1753, when it discovered that it was eleven days ahead of the rest of the world. So England had no choice but to catch up with everyone else, and Parliament ordered the citizenry to drop eleven days of their lives. Well, it created riots in the streets. The people demonstrated outside Parliament thinking this was the government's idea of robbing them of what precious time they had. Yet the people eventually gave in, and the adjustment was finally made. We still have the Julian calendar, and children learn about it through an old Roman saying:

"Thirty days hath September,
April, June, and November.
All the rest have thirty-one,
Except in leap year.
That's when February's days are twenty-nine."

Did you know that many houses throughout England have windows that have been bricked up? You can see some good examples in various parts of London, if you look for them. Well, this was done to avoid paying a "window tax," a very old tax re-introduced by Prime Minister William Pitt. (Incidentally, at twenty-four he was the youngest Prime Minister England has ever seen.) A war with France was brewing that needed financing. (We can't seem to teach the French to leave us alone.) Like many Prime Ministers before him, Pitt scraped the bottom of the money barrel to see what old tax laws were reusable. So the window tax was dug up again. Many people, especially the poor, blocked up lots of windows to avoid paying taxes on them. But when the rich blocked theirs they would commission an artist to paint over the bricked-up window to make it look as if a window was still there. Now, because of the lack of windows this meant the houses were darker inside. So this is where the expression "daylight robbery" comes from.

Did you know that after his separation from the Church of Rome and his marriage to Anne Boleyn, Henry VIII turned his attention to the important matter of dissolving the power of the Catholic Church? He did this by physically destroying the churches, disposing of all the old clergy and replacing them with his own priests, and finally by confiscating their lands. But one or two of the more powerful monastic institutions managed to survive by its inhabitants swearing allegiance to Henry, who therefore kept them under control and collected their revenues.

One of the wealthiest, and therefore strongest, orders was the seat of Glastonbury, which lies in the western part of England. Anyway, the story goes that the abbot there, a Richard Whiting, built himself a fabulous kitchen on the grounds of the abbey. He apparently heard through the grapevine that the King had been informed of his wonderful kitchen, and that he was none too pleased to hear that it was bigger and grander than the King's own at Hampton Court. So fearing retribution, Abbot Whiting attempted to please Henry by having a very large pie baked for him, into which he placed the deeds to twelve valuable estates.

Now, the job of transporting this special pie was given to a man by the name of Jack Horner. It is said that on his way to London, sitting in the corner of the travel wagon with the great pie on his lap, he placed his hand into the pie and pretended to slip out a plum. He promptly pulled out one of the deeds and tucked it into his coat to keep for himself. When he returned to Glastonbury, he told Abbot Whiting that the King himself had given him the deed for delivering his valuable cargo intact to the Crown. The Abbot, although very suspicious, believed Horner, as it was customary to reward a messenger in some way. Or perhaps he thought the King was in a jolly good mood and had simply given Horner one of the deeds without looking at it, even though it was one of the best deeds in the pie. Anyway, Jack Horner came out of the deal quite well. Word apparently got out about his scheme, and a nursery rhyme was created about the whole affair. I expect you know which one is coming up:

> "Little Jack Horner sat in the corner
> Eating his Christmas pie.
> He put in his thumb and pulled out a plum
> And said, 'What a good boy am I!'"

Did you know that one friend of James II was a chap called Judge Jeffrey? It was a name that rang terror in the southwestern part of England. You see, James sent Judge Jeffrey to sort out the Monmouth Rebels, as they were known. This whole affair was recorded in history as the "Bloody Western Circuit." To call this chap a harsh judge was an understatement. The first thing he did was to deport 800 of the Monmouth Rebels to the West Indies and Barbados — no, not for a holiday, but to be used as slaves in the sugar industry. Another 300 fared not as well: they were literally butchered and dangled along the roadside as a warning to others who might get the notion to rebel. Hundreds of people were brought before Judge Jeffrey to be tried, then were later executed without mercy. One woman, upon hearing she was to be hung, appealed to the King, who pardoned her from execution. She was sent for so that Judge Jeffrey could relay to her the King's decision himself. He announced, "The King has granted you a stay of execution by hanging." Then, after a long pause, he continued, "The King said nothing about burning you at the stake." Turning to his subordinates he shouted, "Burn her!"

Judge Jeffrey was appointed Lord Chancellor and so found himself serving close to King James. Yet immediately following the King's overthrow on February 12, 1689, the judge was a little late in packing his bags and joining James in exile in France. He was arrested for his terrible deeds and thrown into the Tower of London. There he was subjected to all sorts of treatment, but he died before he could officially be executed. What a shame.

Did you know that King Henry I was crowned King of England at Westminster Abbey on August 3, 1100, and that he reigned for 35 years and 122 days? Apparently, he was very bad-tempered, just like his brother William II. In fact, his temper was so bad that when he was at Rouen Castle in France, he threw a man over the side of the battlements for breaking his promise of loyalty.

In 1106 his brother Robert showed up from the Crusades. Henry immediately ordered him to come to Cardiff Castle and promptly shut him up in the dungeon for twenty-eight years. You see, now that Robert had returned he was a threat to the Crown; and as long as he was tucked away the Crown was safe.

It was Henry who employed a Roger Salisbury to look after the finances of the kingdom. And it was he who came up with the clever idea of counting out money (such as taxes) on a chequered cloth. By doing this the money could be evenly split: black squares for the country and white squares for the King, so that it was an even fifty-fifty. Or was it? Anyway, the cloth also stopped the coins from slipping through the cracks of the table. This is why even today we call the Finance Minister the Chancellor of the Exchequer.

Now, during the month of November in 1120 Henry was in Normandy (which was also part of his kingdom) with his son William, who he introduced to the barons and nobles as his heir to the throne. This was to make sure that if anything were to happen to the King there would be no doubt in anyone's mind as to who would succeed him. So after all the formal affairs it was time to party. And party these chaps did.

After a few days of revelry, Henry said farewell because his country was waiting for him. Yet his son asked if he could stay another day. The King agreed to this and left his large white ship for William and his mates to return in. Well, tragedy lay ahead. The day William decided to leave, the weather was inclement; the King's captain advised the Prince to delay the crossing. But, following in his father's footsteps, William lost his temper and demanded that the captain take him to England. (I'll bet that if the truth were known, they were all still drunk.) The ship didn't get very far before thick fog made it impossible to see. The vessel then struck a series of rocks that ripped out the bottom and sank like one of those very rocks. Two of the survivors were a butcher from Rouen and the captain, who were hanging onto wreckage for their lives. When the captain asked if the Prince were alive, the butcher told him that William had gone under. Well, the captain muttered that he was not going to outlive the Prince and promptly let go of the wreckage and drowned himself. When the King heard the news, he broke down and wept. He ordered multitudes of people to check the coastline to see if his son or his corpse turned up. It was said that the King never smiled again.

The tragedy for England was that there was no legitimate male heir to the throne — this despite the fact that Henry had fathered more than twenty illegitimate children. All he could offer was his one legitimate daughter, Matilda. To her he left his dominions when he died on December 1, 1122. Of course, right after his death his sister's son Stephen stepped in to become King, and we all know what happened there. But that's another story. (Just a footnote to this story about the white ship. With so many unsolved murders among the English monarchs, there are many people, myself included, who think that perhaps Prince William didn't drown by accident but was in fact murdered. I bet that's got you thinking now.)

Did you know that William II introduced the forest law, which declared that all the forests and woods belonged to the Crown and didn't exist for the commoners' pleasure? A person caught in the woods would be severely punished, and if he shot or killed a deer, well, the poor chap was usually executed on the spot. There were several areas in which commoners could go to collect firewood. And on some days of the year they were allowed to enter certain forests under supervision to knock down branches that overhung the riding paths. (You see, the royals didn't like the branches knocking off their hats, or even themselves from their horses.) The commoners were allowed to use whatever method they wanted, but most of them used a long hook to pull a branch down. Then they would cut it with a crook, which is a very sharp, curved blade, and keep what they had cut. Such is the origin of the saying "by hook or by crook."

Did you know that the cooks for the great Kings and Queens of England were always looking for ways to please their masters? One way they achieved this was to dress up game birds to make them more inviting. A cook would take a pheasant and skin it so that all the feathers were intact. Then when the meat was cooked he would dress it up in its own feathers again so that it would look like a real bird sitting on the King's table. This same procedure was used with swans, geese, guinea fowl — whatever was available.

This sort of dressing-up technique was also done during the reign of Richard II, who at one point, it was reported, had over 2,000 cooks in his employment... except when he was thrown in the Tower of London, where he was starved to death.

Talking about food... did you know that one of Henry VIII's favourite dishes was a baked pie? Now, there were all sorts of pies, but his favourite was a game pie. This consisted of a thick pastry crust at the bottom of the cooking dish, and in that would be the cooked meat of a swan. Inside the swan would be the meat of a duck, inside of which would be a capon, which was filled with a pheasant, which was filled with a grouse. And inside the grouse would be a lark, in whose centre would be a boiled egg. In between the layered meats there was stuffing, cranberries, yellow saffron, liver stuffing, spinach stuffing, and the pastry was put over the top of it all. So when this pie was cut it must have been a colourful sight, fit enough for a King.

Did you know that some of the pies baked many years ago were purely for entertainment purposes, or for a joke to be played on a special guest? The pie crust would be of leather, shaped and dried for the occasion. The contents would be something as unusual as live frogs. The dish would be placed before the King, and when the top was removed the frogs would go leaping everywhere. Even wild cats were used as an ingredient. You can imagine the havoc they caused when the lid was removed.

Remember the nursery rhyme about "four and twenty blackbirds baked in a pie"? Such marvels truly happened. Once there was an enormous pie placed on the table before a feast for King John began at Nottingham Castle. When the cover was removed, four musicians jumped out playing one of the King's favourite tunes. Well, when you think about it, that was considered good live entertainment. There wasn't any television around in those days to ruin their lives.

Did you know that the city of Oxford got its name from the lowest crossing of the River Isis? This river has a name change at Oxford, but it originates in London as the River Thames. Now, the place where a river has a low crossing is called a "ford." So any town or village that ends with the word "ford" had such a crossing at one time. The name "Oxford" was where the farmers drove their oxen across the river: Ox-Ford. Quite a different story for the town of Cambridge: this was simply named after the bridge built over the River Came, hence Came-Bridge. And then there's the name of a city I once lived in:

Stratford-upon-Avon. The name "Strat" is a Saxon word for "Street," which crosses the ford on the River Avon. Thus, we have Strat-Ford-on-Avon. Even today, some people use the word "upon" instead of "on" before "Avon." The reason for this is that historically it was a sort of status symbol, indicating where people lived: either on the river — a house boat, for example — or in a house that sat upon the river.

Did you know that in the early days when the King or Queen travelled around the country it was almost the equivalent of moving a very large army? Almost the entire court travelled: the Lord Great Chamberlain, the Lord High Treasurer, the King's Marshall, and the Keeper of the Seals. Then there were the servants to look after them, including those responsible for feeding the entourage. So you had the poulterers, fruitiers, bakers, confectioners, butlers, several cooks, the keeper of the dishes, the master steward of the larder, and the workmen of the buttery. There were also the chaplains, clerks, lawyers, horn blowers, watchmen, guards, archers, hunters, the keeper of the greyhounds, and even a wolf catcher. And don't forget the keeper of the tents. Also included were the chamberlain of the candles, the water carrier, and the washerwomen to wash everyone's clothes. Then you had all the luggage, pack horses, oxen laden with bags and leather pouches, barrels of coins, boxes of jewels, documents, kitchen equipment, hunting spears, altar cloths, chalices, drinking vessels, quilts, parchment for writing documents, as well as the tables and chairs, the beds (yes, they carried their own beds) and feather pillows, chamber pots (called "goesunder" in those days), and scent bottles. And what about the hangers-on — the scholars, singers, dicers, gamblers, jesters, barbers, and so on. So there were easily over a thousand people who travelled with the monarchs. It was like a plague of locusts going through the country. And when they stopped at a residence the people living there would not only have to entertain the monarchs but look after all the rest of the bunch. In some cases people were made bankrupt after such a visit. (I'll be sure to cross all Kings and Queens off my party list.)

Have you heard about Charles II? His dad was the King who had his head removed by Parliament on January 30, 1649. When Charles was only twelve years old, he was secretly smuggled over to France. He roamed around for eight years plotting and hoping that the Royalists would rise again.

To cut a long story short, Oliver Cromwell died on September 3, 1658. His son Richard succeeded him but was deposed after six months. The English were desperate for the monarchy to return, so a gang of officials was sent over to France to track down Charles. They eventually caught up with him stuffing his face with frog legs and snails. The officials were disgusted and threw up at the sight of this. They told him in no uncertain terms, "Stop eating that crap and you can come back to England and eat fish and chips — civilised food." Well, you know the rest. On May 29, 1660 (his thirtieth birthday — what a great birthday present!), Charles arrived to one tremendous welcome, and after spending some time in Canterbury he arrived in London to a second joyous homecoming. England was now a happy place at last. Or was it? The first thing Charles did was to take revenge on some of the people responsible for the execution of his father, King Charles I. Out of the twenty who were accused he had nine of them executed.

Charles seemed to be forever short of money, and he spent most of his time at the beck and call of France — in the meantime neglecting his own country. On one of his regular trips to France, he stooped so low as to let himself be talked into selling Calais for $400,000 and marrying Catherine of Briganza, daughter of the King of Portugal, for a dowry of $300,000. Charles II reigned for thirty-six years and seven days. He died of uraemia and mercury poisoning. (He should have stayed in France eating those frog legs and snails.)

Did you know that in medieval days beer wasn't brewed as it is today? It was much sweeter. In fact, the main ingredient was fermented apples. Pears were used for a little extra flavour, as were herbs and spices and a touch of honey. So the effects of drinking beer were not as potent today, but it still had a certain kick.

It was recorded in 1632 that children of all ages were given beer to drink. You see, the water was foul. With the lack of hygiene such as it was, everything was dumped into the rivers. And I mean everything. And the wells — well, again, all sorts of nasty business was thrown down them. It was a question of "out of sight, out of mind." But at least beer was boiled. So when you think about it, drinking it made sense.

Did you know that the famous Sir Christopher Wren was asked to submit plans to build a town hall for the town of Windsor? Well, he submitted his plans to the officials, and they all agreed that they were suitable except for one important detail. The officials told Sir Christopher that in his design there were columns all around the base of the building that supported the main structure, but not one column supporting the middle. Sir Christopher explained that this was a new idea and that there was no need for support in the centre. They replied, "We like your design and we will award you the contract. But, for goodness' sake, put some columns in the middle." Sir Christopher agreed.

In short, he constructed the building complete with the columns in the centre just as the officials had requested. But when you find yourself at Windsor and you see this town hall, look at the columns and then check the ones in the middle. They're about an inch short from supporting anything. So Sir Christopher got his own way by building this town hall as he'd originally planned. And for 300 years the centre columns have not been supporting a thing.

Did you know that on August 6, 1762, the first sandwich was born? The story goes that on this day the fourth Earl of Sandwich was busy playing cards when he ordered his servant to put some finger food on the table nearby because he didn't want to be disturbed while luck was in his favour. So the servant got some slices of meat and cheese, plenty of cut bread, and other bits and pieces and left the Earl to it. He placed the items onto a slice of bread and was about to eat it, but the bits and pieces were falling off. So he put another slice of bread over the other one and that seemed to do the trick. His gambling partner also got on well eating like this and so the game continued. The two decided that in the future this would be the food for gaming. After that it was referred to simply as a "sandwich."

So who was this Earl of Sandwich chap? Well, here's a short resumé. In addition to this famous title, he also had another one: First Lord of the Admiralty. But little good he was at that job. Through his incompetent management of the admiralty, he was partly responsible for England losing the American colonies. He experienced the loss of great sums of money through gambling, the loss of his soul to the Devil through being involved in satanic rituals, and the loss of his reputation (such that it was) by consorting with a sixteen-year-old mistress. He lost his life in 1792. And the only thing that we have to remind us of him today is the sandwich.

By the way, the word "sandwich" is of Saxon origin. The first syllable, "sand," meant just what is does today. The second syllable, "wich," meant a jetty into the water, either of sand or rock, or even what we call today a "boardwalk." Hence, the word "sandwich."

Did you know, while we're on the subject of sandwiches, that England's citizens consume over thirteen million sandwiches every day? There are various types of sandwiches made with different types of breads. But apparently the most requested one is the chip butty, despite the fact that you would expect to have cucumber sandwiches at a high-class afternoon tea. So whatever you think of the Earl of Sandwich, as Woody Allen said in the movie *Getting Even*: "He freed mankind from the hot lunch. We owe him that much."

Did you know that outside the Houses of Parliament (the word "Parliament" actually means "talking shop") you'll see three statues? At the entrance is Oliver Cromwell's statue, which was erected in 1899. Now, don't get me wrong — this is a great statue of a great man. But when you think about it, wasn't he the chap who sent in his troops in 1653 and kicked the members of Parliament out then locked the door? Anyway... the other one at the front is the statue of King Richard the Lion Heart, erected in 1860. He was the King who ruled England for ten years and only spent ten months in his own country. He was around about 100 years before there was a Parliament. And he's not even buried in England, so why is his statue out there? And the third one, located on the west side of the building, is a statue of a woman named Emily Pankhurst. She led the campaign for women's suffrage in England. This last statue was erected at the end of the 1920's. Now, she should be at the front, not the other two. (Well, that's my opinion.)

Did you know that the city of London is over 2,000 years old? It was first established as an important town for shipping and supplies by the Romans, who were in England for 400 years. They called it Londinium. The Iceni area of England, which was what is present-day Norfolk and Suffolk, was once ruled by one Prasutagus, who, it was said, was a nice sort of a chap. Well, word has it that the Romans killed Prasutagus and confiscated all his lands in 60 A.D. Now, the Romans didn't know about his wife, who they considered attractive but harmless, and her two beautiful daughters. How wrong they were! This widow, named Queen Boudicca (also known as Boadicea), became a real pain in the neck. She, along with her tremendous following, did everything possible to drive the Romans out of England. She eventually burnt Londinium to the ground, and when the Romans caught her she took her own life by taking poison. (You know, some people are really bad losers.)

In 1666 another great fire broke out in London, but this time it started in a baker's shop belonging to Thomas Faryor, the King's baker in Pudding Lane. He claimed he drew his oven at 10 p.m. on Saturday, September 1, and left a bundle of wet faggots to dry for the purpose of lighting them the next morning. (Faggots are bundles of branches used to get a fire started.) But around midnight he went into the bakehouse to get a light for his candle and found that his oven had burnt out. At 2 a.m. the next morning, Mr Faryor was awakened by his servant, only to find the room filled with smoke. The alarm was given to the rest of the household, and his wife and daughter and the servant escaped by way of a window onto the neighbour's rooftop. But the maid sat paralysed with fear and refused to leave. She was the first victim of the fire.

Then in World War II London was again destroyed by fire, this time by the Germans with their continuous bombing. Over half a million buildings were destroyed and as many lives during these raids. But like the fabled phoenix, the great city of London has repeatedly risen from the ashes.

Talking about London... did you know that in the city limits proper the population is about nine million, but that the majority of the people who inhabit the area live outside the city and that when they commute to work the city's population rises to... get ready for this... twenty million? The total population of the country is fifty-nine million. (And you wonder why you can't find a parking place in the city!)

Did you know that when Cardinal John Fisher, one of Henry VIII's victims, was awakened on the day of his execution and told that the event would take place in four hours, he looked up and smiled, saying, "Good. I can get some more sleep." And he actually had to be awakened again to have his head chopped off. I wonder if he was on something.

Did you know that the sausage is a very old traditional food in England? We serve dishes such as bangers and mash; sausage, egg and chips; toad in a hole; sausage rolls; and sausage sandwiches. Of course, sausages come in all shapes and sizes, from mini-cocktail things to lovely, big, juicy ones. And there are lots of different flavours — even black sausage, which, as far as I'm concerned, is revolting, since the main ingredient is blood.

During World War II, because of rationing, there was a shortage of meat. So sausage manufacturers tended to add more meal and cereal and get away with only a dash of meat. There was also more water in them than you find today. This is why one of our sausages is called "bangers" — because historically while they were cooking the water inside them would boil and explode through the skin.

Did you know, while we're on the subject of sausage, that it's one of the oldest processed foods? The word "sausage" comes from the Latin "salsus," meaning "salted" — in other words, "preserved." There was a reference to the sausage as far back as 500 B.C. when a Greek playwright called Epicarmus even wrote a play called "The Sausage." So long before the ancient Romans, these tasty treats have been around. The Romans were especially fond of sausages. They made them with fresh pork and crushed pine nuts chopped up with cumin, bay leaves, and peppers. Sausages were so popular that they became identified with the early Christian Church. The Emperor Constantine actually banned the eating of sausages in public. Sausage-making became a culinary art in the Middle Ages, and sausages started being named according to the cities where they were produced, for example, Frankfurter, Bologna, Romano, Berliner, and, of course, Salami, believed to be named after the city of Salamis, which is on the east coast of Cyprus.

Did you know that Queen Victoria loved sausages and insisted that the meat in hers be chopped rather than minced and that they should be put into the necessary skins by hand and not by machine? Also, it is said that the present Queen, Elizabeth II, when visiting foreign countries takes large quantities of English bangers with her that she gets from Harrod's. I wonder if she eats them or hands them over as a present. (Maybe that's why we lost the Commonwealth.)

By the way, did you know that we in England consume over 300,000 tons of sausages each year? That works out to roughly twelve pounds per person consumed annually. So they're still banging around.

Did you know that around the fifteenth century many farmers in England started raising sheep? They found it to be more profitable than ordinary farming, since only one shepherd was needed to look after a flock of the creatures. In addition, there was a lot of money to be made in the wool trade. Once the big farmers got the hang of it they would buy out their neighbours and go for even bigger profits. This resulted in very wealthy merchants, which, of course, was profitable for the entire country. So it was only natural for a nursery rhyme to pop up about the subject of wool. And it goes:

"Baa, baa, black sheep, have you any wool?
Yes, sir, yes, sir, three bags full.
One for my master, and one for my dame,
And one for the little boy who lives down the lane."

Did you know that the famous English King named Edward I, known as the "Hammer of the Scots," is buried in Westminster Abbey? But there's more to his demise. While on his deathbed, he got his son Edward (who later became King Edward II) to promise him that when England marched on Scotland his body would be carried ahead of the army, and that when the Scots were finally conquered his body should be put to rest in Scotland. So on a regular basis over the next several years, his body was removed from its tomb and freshly wrapped in oil-soaked linen, just in case there was a campaign. This was done on many occasions, only stopping when King Edward III died on June 21, 1377. The last of Edward I's dynasty ended at that time, so the custom of removing his body from its tomb was neglected and eventually forgotten. In fact, the tomb wasn't opened until 1778, when it was discovered that Edward's body — all six feet two inches of him — was wrapped and preserved. Each bone was individually wrapped quite neatly, each finger was wrapped, as was each hand, each arm, each leg — every part of him was wrapped so painstakingly that his body was well-preserved. And lying on top of his majestic body was his royal robe. It was decided to seal his coffin for good, but not before pouring hot pitch over his entire body so that he could finally be left in peace... By the way, on the side of his tomb is an inscription in Latin that translates as "Here lies Edward I, Hammer of the Scots."

When you visit London and see Trafalgar Square you can't help but notice the enormous Admiralty Arch. It was built fairly recently, in 1911, by Sir Aston Webb as a monument to Queen Victoria. When you've passed through the arch, you'll notice that the road surface changes to a reddish colour. You're now on the Mall, which took its name from the game played by the monarchs called "pall mall." This game was a cross between cricket and golf, and it died out when the monarchs moved from Whitehall. In 1903 the grass was torn up and a new road surface was set in to link up two memorials. The first one honours Queen Victoria and is thirteen feet tall and surrounded by symbolic figures representing Truth, Motherhood, Justice, Science, Art, Naval and Military Power, Progress in Industry, and Victory and Courage. It stands outside Buckingham Palace and is known as a very busy statue, in that there's so much to view and still it's difficult to see it all. The second one is the previously mentioned Admiralty Arch, another Victorian monument.

As you go down the Mall from the Palace, you'll notice a row of mansions on your left that have housed princes and aristocrats. The first one is called Lancaster House. It was built in 1825 for the Duke of York, who died without notice before paying for it. Chopin played for Queen Victoria in the music room. The house has changed hands many times. The next mansion is called Clarence House, the home of the Queen Mother. This house was taken over by the Royal Family in 1952 when Elizabeth II took over as Queen of England. It's not open to the public, but the Queen Mother comes to the gate to wave to the public on her birthday, August 4. Both Lady Diana and Sarah Ferguson stayed here on the eve of their weddings. Behind Clarence House is St James' Palace, which is well worth a visit. (The Mall, incidentally, is a good spot to watch the changing of the guard.)

Talking about royal residences... Buckingham Palace was named after the Duke of Buckingham. He had this country house built... well, in the country. Yes, this whole area was made up of fields and woodlands at the time. (And just look at it now.) The building was constructed in 1703. Now, the story goes that the Duke was not very good at paying his way. In fact, he was constantly short of funds. When the house was near completion, his architect, who was also his builder, spent a considerable amount of his own money to finish the project. One day the architect went to the Duke to collect his fee and, knowing how the Duke tried to avoid paying on time, he invited the Duke to accompany him to the roof to show him the view — or that's what he said. When they were both on the roof, the architect shut the door to it, locked the door with the only key, held it above his head, and walked over to the edge of the roof. By now the Duke was terrified, wondering what on earth the architect was going to do. The architect told the nobleman in a very stern voice that if the Duke didn't sign a banker's order immediately he would throw himself off the roof with the key, leaving the Duke stranded. The architect further explained that he hadn't received any money from him — the Duke — lately, and that if he didn't receive payment soon he would be financially ruined. And so he might just as well end it all. Well, the Duke didn't hesitate in writing out a banker's order. And that's how Buckingham House got started.

But when did it become a royal residence? In 1762 King George III purchased the house and had bits built on to it, but he never actually lived there. Then George IV had a go of it and added a bit here and there. Later came Queen Victoria, who added her bit to the place, then in 1837 she actually decided to move in. Thus, she was, in fact, the first member of royalty to take up residence in this now city dwelling, although it was once a country house. So this is why we now call it Buckingham Palace after the Duke of Buckingham.

While we're on the subject of Queen Victoria... did you know that she married Prince Albert of Saxe-Coburg-Gortha on February 10 (my own birthday, coincidentally) in the year 1840 and that they had four sons and five daughters? She adored her young, handsome husband, and when he died in 1861 at the age of forty-two she was overcome with grief. She shut herself up in Windsor Castle and refused to appear in public for many years, thus becoming known as the Black Widow of Windsor. Albert's death was blamed on the drains at Windsor Castle. Apparently, sewage had been seeping into the water supply, and Albert had habitually drunk lots of water.

The Prince had designed Victoria's beloved Isle of Wight residence, called Osborne House. It is said that the staff were instructed to leave the Prince's personal items exactly where he had left them before his demise. His butler was also instructed to lay out the Prince's clothes every day. A place was even set for him at the dining table. In addition, Victoria had marble hands of Albert and marble feet of her children made, which she kept under her pillow.

Yet during her reign Victoria ruled over an empire that consisted of one-quarter of all the land in the world and the people who lived there. Trade and industrial drive made Victorian Great Britain the world's richest nation. In fact, anything made in England was very much in demand. She died at Osborne House on January 22, 1901. Having reigned for 63 years and 216 days, she holds the record for the longest-reigning monarch.

Did you know that although most of Europe was Catholic long before King Henry VIII made his break with Rome, there were many people who were fed up to the teeth with the Pope? One of the more vocal among them was a chap by the name of Martin Luther, a German priest who also criticised the Pope and didn't agree with either the beliefs of the Catholic Church or the ceremonies it was conducting. He wanted major reforms, so this movement was known as the Reformation. Martin Luther had many followers throughout Europe who agreed with him, and these people became known as Protestants.

Have you ever wondered about the origin of some of our nursery rhymes? Take this one, for instance:

"Sing a song of six pence, a pocket full of rye,
Four and twenty blackbirds baked in a pie.
When the pie was opened the birds began to sing.
Wasn't that a dainty dish to set before the King?

The King was in his counting house counting all his money.
The Queen was in the parlour eating bread and honey.
The maid was in the garden hanging out the clothes,
When down came a blackbird and pecked off her nose."

Well, the interpretation I like involves King Henry VIII. When Henry decided to dissolve the monasteries, his advisor, Thomas Cromwell, suggested that he sell off the properties that went with them. Being short of money, the King snapped up the idea and kept the money for himself. But this also meant that a lot of choir members and other people connected with the monasteries were out of a job. So, if you study the rhyme, you'll see it refers to the twenty-four famous choirs from selected monasteries that were disbanded; the King who was in his counting house counting the revenue from the sales of property; the Queen who was busy looking after herself, no doubt feeding her face; and the maids who were in the garden gossiping about the person lurking in the background waiting to snap up the King, right under Queen Catherine of Aragon's nose. Who else but Anne Boleyn?

William Shakespeare invested money not only in property and land but in the theatre. During 1597 the company called the Lord Chamberlain's Men had a dramatic change. The lease on their theatre ran out. But to crown it all, the key patron, James Burbidge, had died unexpectedly — or, as the saying goes, without notice. Then, after some drawn-out discussions, the two sons of Burbidge, Richard and Cuthbert, decided to dismantle the theatre. So other supporters of the Chamberlain's Men chipped in and moved the theatre by boat across the Thames and set it up opposite St Paul's Cathedral at Southwark and next to the Bear Garden, not far away from The Swan. The records show that Shakespeare had invested eighty pounds of his own money in the theatre, now called The Globe — or, to use Bill's own phrase in *Henry V*, "this wooden O."

In those days, a person paying to see a performance put his money in a strong box. No change was given; the coin was simply passed through a slot in the lid — one penny for the open pit, two pennies for the gallery, and three pennies for a seat with a cushion. When the play started, the box with the money was taken away to a strong room called the "box office," a term we still use today.

Incidentally, theatregoers were never surprised about what kind of play was about to be performed. A black flag flying on top of the theatre indicated that the play was a tragedy, a white flag that it was a comedy.

As we all know from the early history of the Kings and Queens, they had a very hard time obtaining funds from Parliament to wage war on people like the French. So crushing taxes were often levied on the people of England, thus driving the have-nots even further into poverty. (History has a habit of repeating itself.) But this system was to experience a dramatic change, due to the efforts of a Scottish financier named William Peterson. He founded what is now the greatest financial institution in the world, called, simply, the Bank of England.

Now, in order to raise 1.5 million pounds to lend to the British government at 8 percent interest when King William II wanted funds from Parliament to go to war with — who else? — the French, Peterson actually began writing promissory notes by hand. Then a charter was granted on July 27, 1694. And so from that point on, the Bank of England has been the government's banker and debt collector.

In 1797 the Prime Minister, William Pitt, "frequently demanded gold"; and, just like the press today, the newspapers had a go at him, depicting him as an old lady wrapped in bank notes sitting on a padlocked Bank of England money chest. The titles of this illustration were "Political Ravishment" and — the most famous — "The Lady of Thread Needle Street in Danger." The bank still retains the second nickname even today.

Today the bank is in the centre of the city's financial district and is considered very safe, which wasn't the case in 1836. The basement goes down three levels, and the story goes that a man who worked in the city's sewer system actually made his way into the gold bullion vaults but never touched a thing — the fool! Although a few gold bars would have gotten him out of the sewers, he told the bank officials what he'd accomplished, and for his honesty they rewarded him with 800 pounds. Do you know that one 28-pound gold bar is worth 100,000 pounds? This sewer chap needed to clean up his act.

In 1994 the Bank of England minted a special two-pound coin to celebrate 300 years of banking. When you're in England, have a look for this coin. It will be a collector's item in the future.

Did you know that Robert the Bruce, King of Scotland (1306–1329), was a bit of a villainous character before he was King? To explain... Robert the Bruce was the son of Robert Bruce, who was the Earl of Garrick. He had the reputation of being a ruthless individual, and, like many early Scots, he fervently disliked the English. The story goes that in 1306 Robert the Bruce brutally murdered John Comyn, a cousin of King John, in a church, apparently by throwing him onto the altar and stabbing him to death. Now, this was not only murder but sacrilege as well, due to the act and the place. The penalty undoubtedly would have been public execution. But — and here is the twist to this story — to avoid any blame or punishment Robert the Bruce immediately proclaimed himself King of Scotland. By doing this he was free of any conviction or punishment. (Once again, another case of history repeating itself: If you have wealth or a good position in life, then you can get away with murder.)

While we're on the subject of Scotland, did you know that country's early people were called Picts? This was the name given to an early Celtic-speaking tribe by the Romans. It means "painted people." By the late sixth century there was only one kingdom of the Picts, yet for a time they dominated the whole of Scotland. By the ninth century, though, they had weakened considerably from being repeatedly raided by Norse tribes. It was during one of these frequent raids that the Scottish Picts were caught sleeping during the middle of the night after a very long battle. These Viking characters were creeping up on them in a surprise attack, having removed their footwear so they wouldn't be detected. What they didn't realise was that the entire area was thick with large Scottish thistles, and, fortunately for the Scots, the noise the Norsemen made treading on the plants awakened them. Thus, they were saved by the thistle, and that's why the Scots proudly display it as their country's emblem.

Remember King Henry V? Well, when he won the tremendous victory at Agincourt in 1415, he was not only King of England but now also heir to the throne of France. And to seal the deal he married the French King's daughter, Catherine of Valois, known in Shakespeare's *Henry V* as Little Kate. Anyway, when Henry died in Vincennes Castle near Paris on August 31, 1422 (on a Wednesday, and it was raining), Catherine remarried, this time to Owen Tudor. (By the way, two generations later the Tudor family inherited the throne.)

When Catherine died thirty-seven years later, she was buried in the east end of Westminster Abbey. Then King Henry VII came along and decided to have a chapel built in his honour in that part of the abbey. It was pointed out to him that people were in fact buried there. Yet his orders were to move them. So Catherine's body was dug up and stuck to one side of the abbey until someone could decide what to do with her. (Are you still with me?) Now, when you think about this, here you have a loose coffin just sitting off to one side of Westminster Abbey, and inside it lies the daughter of King Charles VI of France, the wife of King

Henry V, the mother of King Henry VI, and the grandmother of King Henry VII — just lying around like a piece of lost luggage for over 200 years.

Now, what I'm leading up to is that the famous diarist Samuel Pepys (1633–1703) decided to make inquiries about this very coffin. When the verger of the abbey revealed who it was, Pepys gave him a very handsome tip to open it up. The two of them unwrapped the top part of the body and peeled off the linen cloth around her face. And there before them was the well-preserved, leathery face of Catherine of Valois. Pepys got on his knees, leaned over her face, and kissed her on the cheek. When he arrived home, he wrote in his famous diary: "I reflected that this was my birthday, thirty-six years old, and I did first kiss a Queen." Well, not long after this, someone in the abbey decided to do some tidying up. So at last Catherine was moved to her final resting place, the chancery of her husband Henry V. But I suppose they're still not really together, for she's on top and he lies at the bottom. Have a look for this when you visit the famous Westminster Abbey.

Did you know that in December 1759 a thirty-four-year-old man named Arthur Guinness signed a 9,000-year lease with an annual rent of forty-five pounds to take over an old brewery called St James Gate? It had stood idle for over ten years. The beverages of choice in Ireland at the time were mainly whiskey, gin, and poteen. The beer that was drunk was imported. So when Guinness started brewing he had to compete with the big-name porter beers from London. He not only competed but virtually ran them out of Ireland. And by 1769 he'd started exporting his own porter beer, which has become a household name worldwide.

Did you also know that Dublin, the capital of Ireland, has a population of over three million and that the total amount of Guinness drunk there per day is two million pints? They claim that one pint of Guinness is equivalent to a six-ounce steak. Well, all I can say is, Dubliners certainly like their steaks.

What follows deals with a subject that most people know something about. But have a look at my own interpretation. During the reign of Elizabeth I, the Church had enormous power over peoples' lives. You had to get permission to marry someone; you couldn't leave your town or village without the permission of a Church official; you were even told what you could eat on which days of the week. And if you didn't comply, then you were punished in one of a variety of ways. At one point heavy fines were in fashion, and if you couldn't pay or you protested the fine then off to prison you went. The religious persecution that took place during this period had a great impact on the people of England. Many families didn't agree with the way the Church was being run and stayed away from it in protest.

When Elizabeth died on March 24, 1603, at the age of sixty-nine, King James I became King of England and Scotland. And things didn't get any better. The Nonconformists were shown no mercy at all. The penalties got even "wors-er-er" (a word of my own invention, meaning "if it doesn't get better then it's worse than it was, so it's "wors-er-er"). This is what prompted a number of families who could afford it to move across the English Channel to Holland and away from the persecution taking place in England. Understandably, it was during this period that many people began to discuss starting a new life in order to live their own way without being persecuted by the monarchy. So they set their sights on the New World.

Lo and behold, King James granted them permission to form a settlement in the New Land. Well, it took about three years to plan the voyage. The Nonconformists decided who would go. Then those who were to make the voyage had to sell most of their worldly goods to help raise funds to get the show on the road. The transportation they located was called... no, it was called the *Speedwell*. When they purchased this ship, obviously somebody didn't kick the tyres on it and... well, you'll see. On July 20, 1620, the *Speedwell* left Holland and headed for Southampton to join up with the gang from England, who were boarding the other ship, called the *Mayflower*.

Both groups finally set off on August 15, 1620, but things didn't go too well for the *Speedwell*. The only speed that was happening involved the amount of water pouring in from several places in the ship's hull. So the crew pulled into the naval port of Plymouth. There the *Speedwell* was dumped. The passengers who happened to have the most resources joined those already on board the *Mayflower*. Finally, all was ready for the day of departure, September 6, 1620, for the 150 passengers, 35 Nonconformists, and 66 adventurers, along with servants and crew. The *Mayflower* unfurled its sails and pointed west, heading for TEXAS. (Just joking.)

If you find yourself in Plymouth, in the area called the Barbican, you can visit the site where the *Mayflower* left for the promised land. There's a pub called the The Crowns, which was serving customers when the Pilgrims set sail. They very possibly had a pint of beer at this pub before leaving. You might want to try one yourself.

Did you know that in the early days of stagecoach travel passengers used to carry small amounts of money in a special purse, just in case they were stopped and robbed? Highway robbery was at times simply pesky for travellers; other times, no mercy was spared when they were caught.

A few individuals were quite good at this crime. For example, Dick Turpin was known as a notorious highwayman. He once tried to put a woman on an open fire when she wouldn't hand over her money. He was eventually captured and hung in York. When you visit this city, you can still see the tyburn where he was hung, located near the present-day racecourse. Another renowned highwayman was called John Ran-Sixteen String-Jack. He was once a coachman and footman, only five feet five inches tall, but he was always dressed immaculately. His name derived from his custom of wearing sixteen silk scarf ribbons tied to the knee of his breeches. He also wore a heavily embroidered scarlet coat, a silk waistcoat, white silk stockings, and a fancy laced hat. He was obsessed with robbing the rich and took great pride in his approach and appearance. Well, just like Turpin, Mr Ran-Sixteen

String-Jack got caught, in 1774, after robbing a clergyman of his silver watch near London. He was found guilty and was to be executed. When he arrived on the scaffold to suffer his punishment, he was wearing a brand-new suit of pea green velvet, a hat with bands of silver wrapped around it, a shirt with a ruffle of lace, and a big flower arrangement in one of his buttonholes. He must have looked a right spectacle. The highwayman showed no remorse for his deeds and was hung to the loud cheers of the crowd.

By the way, a tyburn was a site where hangings took place. It was named after the large tyburn in London that stood where Marble Arch is today. The word "tyburn" came from the River Tyburn that once ran through London and connected with the River Thames but was blocked off during the seventeenth century. (Another river was also blocked off and a famous street named after it: Fleet Street.)

In that magnificent cathedral at Canterbury you can visit the spot where Thomas Becket, Archbishop of Canterbury, was murdered. Now, this is a story that echoes through English history and has always attracted people from many corners of the world.

Becket was later made a saint, and his shrine was of particular interest to sick people, who visited it in hopes of being healed. Not many people know that one of the visitors to the shrine was King Louis of France. He was hoping the powers of Becket could heal his son, who apparently was quite ill. As a gift to the saint, the King placed his most precious jewel, known as the Regal of France, on the shrine. It remained at Canterbury for nearly 400 years. Then in 1539, when Henry VIII came along during the Reformation, he seized the stone, claiming that Becket was a fraud. Henry had it cut up and made into rings.

So, what happened on that infamous day of Tuesday, December 29, 1170? Henry II had put Thomas Becket in the powerful position of Archbishop of Canterbury because he was having trouble with the Church. And to have an old mate of his running the show he, the King, could get all sorts of things done. Right? Wrong. Becket became so engrossed with his work that when the King would ask him to do something for him, he, Becket, would often decline. This really got up the King's nose. Here was Becket doing the opposite of what the King had put him there for. Well, Henry got sick as a parrot about the state of affairs.

Then one day Becket was in London and the King asked him, being old mates as they were, for a favour. Becket refused to help the King and went storming off back to Canterbury. The King was fuming, and in a fit of anger he cried out those famous words: "Will no one rid me of this turbulent priest?" Four of Henry's loyal knights mounted their horses and rode to Canterbury Cathedral. They arrived to locked doors. Their pounding brought no response; the monks refused to open them. Then echoing through the cathedral came the voice of Becket: "I will not have the church a castle." And he ordered his monks to open up the doors. With the four knights ganging up on Becket, he uttered his final words in answer to his accusers: "I am not a traitor, but the Archbishop and a priest of God." Kneeling nearby was a monk named Grim, who recalled Becket's last words: "Into Thy hands, O Lord, I commend my spirit." And as the four knights carried out their deed, Becket was heard to murmur: "For the name of Jesus, and the defence of the Church, I am willing to die." Thus, the Archbishop of Canterbury was brutally murdered.

You can see where all this took place. But remember that the original cathedral burnt to the ground. So the spot you'll be looking at is believed to be near the actual site of Becket's murder.

Did you know that Queen Victoria was only eighteen when she became Queen of England on June 20, 1837? She had four sons and five daughters: Victoria, Alice, Albert, Helena, Louise, Arthur, Leopold, Beatrice, and Alfred. She was the first woman to use chloroform to ease the pain of childbirth. She was also nicknamed the "Grandmother of Europe" because of the fact that her children married Europeans.

By the way, Victoria's eldest daughter, who was also a Victoria but was known as Vicky, got married in 1858 to the future Emperor of Germany, which automatically gave her the grand title of Empress of Germany. Well, when Queen Victoria heard about this, she really was not amused since her daughter would outrank her, being a mere Queen as she was. Benjamin Disraeli, the Prime Minister at the time, worked hard to push a Royal Titles Bill through an unwilling House of Commons. In fact, the bill promoted the Queen to the higher position of Empress of India. This was purely for India, but the Queen virtually appointed herself to the higher position of Empress of the

Commonwealth, a title that put her in command of more than 400 million people. (Well, now she certainly outranked her daughter, who was only Empress of Germany.)

In later life Henry VIII grew grotesquely fat and suffered agonizingly from the severe pain caused by the weeping ulcers on his leg. His weight made him physically helpless, and he had to be moved around with the aid of machinery and numerous attendants. Because of all this, he became increasingly irrational, irritable, bad-tempered, and dangerous. He eventually died on January 27, 1547 (it was Wednesday, and it was raining). After a three-week wait for the tomb to be prepared, his body was taken on a long procession to its final resting place at St George's Chapel in Windsor Castle. While his coffin was being moved about, it burst open on the chapel floor. The foul fat and putrefied blood and blubber crept its way around the floor, bringing people to their knees with the smell. The attendants gathered up the mess as best they could and put him back in his large wooden box. "Bury me next to my sweet Jane" had been his orders, and thus he was placed next to his third wife, Jane Seymour. She was the one who had given him his only son, Edward VI, though she died in the process. When you visit Windsor Castle, you can see Henry VIII's tomb, as well as the splendour of St George's Chapel.

Did you know that chemical warfare is nothing new? In medieval days, during the great sieges of castles and other fortifications, heated sand was used to throw at the knights in shining armour, which penetrated the joints and caused great problems. Even more commonly used were boiling water and boiling animal fats. (Now, that would send me straight home.) There has also been talk of boiling lead, but we haven't much evidence to back those stories up. After all, that's very heavy stuff to throw around — plus, it was a costly product. Powdered quicklime was used quite a lot in the early days, even, it was recorded, on the tips of arrowheads. Even more sneaky was its use at the entrance of a castle. Next time you're about to enter, say, Warwick Castle you'll pass through the portcullis gate (the heavy gate that's raised and lowered). Look up and you'll see holes in the ceiling. These apertures are called murder holes, and that's exactly what they were used for. You see, once a person passed through the portcullis it was dropped behind him. Then to get into the castle he had to pass through another one, which was also lowered. In other words, he was trapped. Now, if the owners of the castle didn't like this visitor, they could drop all sorts of stuff down on him through the murder holes, including the very effective quicklime. So, once again, history repeats itself — this time in the case of chemical warfare.

Did you ever think about what was used in early days for windows? Well, the word for "window" comes from "wind hole," and that's exactly what it was — a hole that would allow air and light through. At night a roll of animal hide would be hung over the hole, with rocks holding it down, and in the daytime it would be rolled up out of the way. Now, if you were to keep saying the words "wind hole" over and over again, it would eventually sound just like "window."

In medieval days, if you were a high ranker you wouldn't have a common skin over your window. Instead, you'd roll out the horns of animals that had been fused together. This would let light in and certainly keep out the wind. But, even better, you'd have a type of shutters over your windows.

Now, during the Norman period glass was being used, but mainly only in the cathedrals. And of course the rich could afford it, so castles and manor houses were fitted with it. Henry III introduced glass in all his great halls and castles. He even had it in his privy chambers. But glass was so valuable that if the residents went away for a long period of time, it was a common practise to remove the glass and hide it until they returned.

While we're on the subject of castles... did you know that at Christmas time the banqueting and feasting went on for days and sometimes weeks? For example, in 1206 King John spent Christmas at Winchester Castle, and orders were given to the Sheriff of Hampshire to round up the following food: 2,000 chickens, 5,000 eggs, 20 oxen, 200 pigs, and 200 sheep. The records also show an almost endless supply of wine. Tons of bread was prepared, along with a tremendous number of desserts. So if you were in the King's favour you could be guaranteed a great Christmas feast.

Now, several days before the feasting was to begin, the King would go out hunting with his huntsmen, who were always paid at the more than adequate rate of about eight pennies a day. The head huntsman would normally be at least a knight in the King's party. (King John had a least four head huntsmen.) At the head of the hunt would be four hornblowers, about twenty sergeants (who were, in fact, beaters), several assistant huntsmen, a variety of dog handlers, a troop of mounted wolf hunters, many crack archers, and, finally, one personal archer, who would assist the King and carry his bow — a bit like a caddie. So a royal hunt was just like a small military expedition.

In the early times the lords' and ladies' chambers, when situated on the upper floor, were known as the solar. In fact, any private chamber, irrespective of its location, was called a solar. Its principal item of furniture was the great wooden four-poster bed with a heavy frame. The supports invariably were thick ropes, but the really posh might have twisted leather ropes. The mattress was a canvas bag filled with all types of feathers, somtimes mixed with wool. The pillows were filled with the same. Sheets were seldom used; much more common were quilts and fur blankets for the cold. (By the way, when members of the nobility travelled, they very often took their own beds with them. This was to ensure a good night's sleep. In addition, a bed was also considered a personal item — royalty didn't like sharing beds in those days.) The beds were curtained with a heavy fabric that was pulled back during the day and closed at night. Now, there were two reasons for closing themselves in the bed: either they needed to keep out the cold in the winter, or they wanted to have privacy. You might think, "But why didn't they close the door to the room for privacy?" Well, it wasn't like that. You see, their personal servants would sleep in the same room, in case their master or mistress wanted something during the night. The servants wouldn't sleep so cosily either — on a bench, on the floor, or, if they were lucky, on a trundle bed. The other part of a noble person's bed was the canopy. This kept off all the bugs and creepy crawlies that fell from the thatch roof. Rats and mice also often fell, since they loved living in the straw. So now you know not to sleep with your mouth open while in a bed without a canopy under a thatch roof.

Did you know that the town of Brighton was originally known as Brighthelmstone? During that time it was a sleepy little town with not much going on. Then a man named Dr Richard Russell published a book explaining the benefits of not only sea air but also of bathing in the sea. This had previously been unheard of — the sea was just for looking at. "You mean to say, actually go into the sea?" people asked in disbelief. When they understood that the answer was affirmative, the floodgates were opened (figuratively speaking), and thousands of people went to visit Brighthelmstone. Enough of them fell sufficiently in love with the place that the town was soon booming. People from all sorts of places were moving there, including George, the Prince of Wales. So if it was good enough for a prince... well, even more people uprooted themselves from the inland areas and headed for the coast.

Prince George, who by now was a frequent visitor to the resort town, started secretly seeing a woman by the name of

Maria Fitzherbert. Now it might have been all right for the Prince to go out on a date, but in this case it had to be in secret because the woman was a Catholic. And it was out of order for a royal personage to get mixed up with Catholics. It wasn't long before the Prince set his sights on staying in Brighthelmstone. So he built a whacking great big fancy palace called the Brighton Pavilion and, because he couldn't get this woman into bed, the Prince married her, without his father's permission. So what he had done was to ignore the Royal Marriage Act.

Then the entire affair became the worst-kept secret — in fact, what with all the rumours flying around London, he caused a right royal scandal. (So what's new?) He was building up enormous debts furnishing his own residence, called Carlton House. He'd already been given 30,000 pounds by Parliament and was getting 50,000 pounds from his dad; yet he ran up a debt of over 250,000 pounds (which in today's terms would be several millions). But with his charm and a promise to get rid of Maria Fitzherbert, he managed to squeeze even more money from Parliament.

What remains to be told about the Prince is another story. But to finish up about this famous seaside town... people got fed up with calling it Brighthelmstone and abbreviated it to its present name of Brighton. As for Maria Fitzherbert, well, she must have done all right. She ended up as one of the few people to go down in history of having died during a fit of laughing. (You can visit the Brighton Pavilion, as it's still called, when you go to this now bustling town south of London. Incidentally, Brighton has the first nude beach in the country. What a pleasant town to visit.)

Not far from Brighton is a town called Portsmouth, known as the birthplace of the British Navy. Actually, it was Henry V who established the first fleet in 1415 (although it's recorded that King Alfred had formed a navy during his reign of 871–899). One of the most famous naval personnel in Portsmouth was Admiral Lord Nelson, who, on September 14, 1805, walked proudly through the streets of Portsmouth to cheering crowds and well-wishers en route to boarding his famous flagship, the *H.M.S. Victory*. Nelson was very popular with ordinary people, despite all the rumours about his having an affair with the loverly Lady Hamilton. Five weeks after leaving Portsmouth he destroyed the Spanish fleet at Trafalgar. But while surveying the destruction, a sniper from a crippled Spanish ship mortally wounded him on the deck of his own ship. He died shortly thereafter. His monument stands in the square named after this famous battle: Trafalgar Square, which you can see on your visit to London.

By the way, did you know that Nelson's body was put in a barrel of brandy to preserve it for its long journey home? (I wonder what they did with the brandy once he was taken out.)

Did you know that when Elizabeth I died, because she'd never married nor had children she left no direct descendent for the throne? So one of those unusual situations of "Who do we give the gold hat to?" presented itself. The only person directly in line was the son of Mary, Queen of Scots. If you remember, she was the one whose head was removed by the order of her half-sister, Elizabeth I. So, there it was: King James VI of Scotland on his way to London with his wife, Anne of Denmark, to be crowned King of England on July 25, 1603. Thus, he also became King James I of England, and both England and Scotland were united to become one country. (That's why we call it the United Kingdom.)

James I was known as "the wisest fool in Christendom." He wrote a book warning the general public about witches — a subject that fascinated him. He was also gay, despite his marriage (which was nothing new among some of the royalty). He had a number of favourites, one of them being George Villiers, whom he promoted to be the Earl of Buckingham. To show how much he was affected by this chap, here are quotes from one of the many letters he wrote to George: "God bless you, my child and wife... "; he signed it: "Your dear dad and husband, James." (No comments, please.) Now, although King James was a Protestant like most of the people of England, his mother, if you remember, was a Catholic, and England still persecuted Catholics, which naturally caused friction between the two religions. The Protestants thought James might change the official religion back to Catholicism in revenge for their having executed his mother. But this was not to be; James remained a Protestant. So a group of Catholic conspirators got together, headed by Sir Robert Catesby, Robert Winter, John Wright, and Guy Fawkes, and planned to blow up Parliament at the State opening on November 5, 1605, when King James would be present. They loaded up the basement under the House of Lords with thirty barrels of gunpowder, which they had smuggled in by means of a tunnel from the building next door. The plot was uncovered when a Catholic member of Parliament was handed an anonymous letter. Guy Fawkes was the leading light, if you like: he was the one caught lighting the fuse. While being held and tortured in the Tower of London, he confessed the names of the other conspirators, who were later caught and also executed. So the King was saved.

But before long His Majesty was getting on the nerves of the members of Parliament by claiming the "divine right of Kings." What this meant was that he believed that all his thoughts and orders came directly from God. He actually did away with Parliament and ran the country with some of his courtiers and his favourite people. One of his schemes to raise funds was to invent a new title called a baronet. He sold this off to whomever could afford it for 1,000 pounds.

James I was a serious eater — a glutton, really. In 1625 he developed a nasty stomach bug, though the rumour circulated that he had been poisoned. (This is the story that I believe.) Yet his death was diagnosed as kidney failure, caused by the excessive consumption of food and wine. James had started out being a fine chap but sadly ended up a disaster by the time he died on March 27, 1625. His first son, another James, who died of typhoid, was succeeded by his second son Charles, who became known as Charles I.... But that's another story.

Stratford-on-Avon has a tremendous number of old places to visit. Most of them are connected with William Shakespeare; but there's one famous house that isn't, though it's not far from the place where the playwright died. Harvard House is a unique, richly carved, half-timbered house that's well worth a visit. It was the home of Catherine Rogers, mother of John Harvard, the chap who moved to America in 1637 because of the religious persecution rampant in England at the time, and founded Harvard University the following year. (By the way, the house was presented to Harvard University in 1909 by a man named Edward Morris from Chicago.)

The house, an unusually large one for the period, was built in 1596. Upstairs is the main bedroom in which the mother and father slept. (In the United States, it would be called the master bedroom.) Going to any other room upstairs meant going through that room, which in turn meant that the parents could monitor the coming and going of their children. (Parents were very strict in those days.) The children were also segregated: the girls slept at one end of the house and the boys at the other end. Only the girls had beds; the boys slept on hay and straw thrashings.

In the parents' room there's an unusual piece of furniture called a Bible chair. During the reign of Elizabeth I, anti-Protestant laws made it illegal to own a family Bible. So the idea behind this special chair was to hide the Bible in a secret compartment, in case there was a random search of the house. When such a search took place, the lady of the house would sit down in the chair and, what with the large flowing dress she wore, would conceal the entire chair. Since it wasn't polite to ask a lady to rise to her feet, the chair would end up saving the family Bible, an asset valuable to the family not only for its religious significance, but also because of the recording of births, marriages, and deaths made at the back of the book.

One afternoon some time during the 1880's a man named John and his girlfriend named Rosalyne were in a boat on the famous Loch Lomand in Scotland. "Well," you might ask, "what's so special about that?" During those Victorian days it was not the done thing for a respectable young lady to be accompanied by a man without the assistance of a chaperone. And that's what the problem was with this afternoon's outing of a picnic on a remote island. The very unattractive, and very unwanted, chaperone was called Winafred. John schemed up an idea to get rid of her. He aimed his boat at one small island, pulled alongside it, and asked the chaperone to go ashore to catch the rope. But as soon as she was ashore he pushed the boat away with his oar and sailed off to another romantic-looking island. There he had a splendid picnic with his young lady in the peace and quiet that was befitting his style. The two of them eventually set off to pick up the still screaming chaperone, and the chap took them both home.

The reason I've told you this story is that the young man in question was the famous mapmaker named John Bartholomew. At some point before the picnic, he'd been mapping out Loch Lomand and had noticed that two little islands he'd visited had no name. So, following the successful picnic, he named one after his girlfriend Rosalyne and the other after her chaperone Winafred.

Did you know that Charles Dickens visited Stratford-on-Avon in 1838? Actually, he had a drink and lunch next door to Shakespeare's birthplace, which was a pub called The Swan & Maidenhead. This building had once been the business premises of John Shakespeare, William's father. Charles was with his great travelling friend with the rare hyphenated name, Hever-Lock-Knight-Brown (better known as "Fizz"), who also illustrated his novels. They were both fascinated by William Shakespeare's plays and sonnets, and after visiting the playwright's house they signed the visitors' book, which is on view. Their visit was very fortunate, in my opinion, because in 1847 Shakespeare's birthplace came up for sale. And guess who was trying to make a deal? Mr Barnham of circus fame. He wanted to purchase the house of our Bill and ship it over to America "brick by brick," as the saying goes, to set it up in a museum. Well, when Charles Dickens happened to hear about this he was furious. The result of his fury was that a bunch of dignitaries all chipped in their funds and purchased the house.

This act was the beginning of the Shakespeare Trust. Those same dignitaries later purchased all the other properties associated with Bill to make sure they wouldn't end up in the wrong hands — or even in the wrong country.

The Vikings were great traders of fur and amber. They also excelled at travelling impressive distances in their great boats. Logically, they managed to pop up on all four corners of England, it being an island. Apart from bringing their goods to trade, there was another thing that came along with just about all their visits, and that was fear. They certainly lived up to their name ("Viking" means "pirate") because they plundered, pillaged, and raped any defenceless region they happened to come across. And England was no exception along their trail of terror. Many towns and villages still bear the names these marauders gave them. For example, York was once a thriving Viking town called Yorvik.

In Europe two major breakaway groups from these Viking settlers formed their own countries. One of these was called the Russ group; they eventually formed what we know today as Russia. The second breakaway group — surprising to many people — was the Normans. Yes, those early settlers were in fact Vikings. So you can see where both countries got their taste of conquering from.

Did you know that every year in London, even in the twentieth century, a medieval court case called the Trial of the Picks takes place? To explain... this particular trial goes right back to the year 1248, and its purpose is to test the coins of the realm. So, you see, the only thing really on trial is the newly minted coins. The money is brought directly from the Royal Mint in special boxes called "picks." Each box contains separate bags of coins of a different value. The coins have been picked at random and are tested by the jury. Proceeding over the jury is the Queen's Remembrancer — what you would call the remains of the Exchequer. This ancient act dates back to when the coins were tried before the Barons of the Exchequer. It is a case of testing the quality and perfection of the coins, and, yes, the coins actually go on trial. It's obvious that some old traditions in England are just hard to give up.

Did you know that the members of the royal family of England have had an amazing assortment of animals presented to them over the past twenty years by heads of states during their visits around the world? For example, the Duke of Edinburgh was given two hippopotamuses by the president of Liberia. (Well, they were the pygmy version, so I suppose he could have trained them to fetch a stick on the grounds of Buckingham Palace.) The Soviet leader, Nikita Khruschev, gave Princess Anne a brown bear called Nicky. Prince Edward was presented with a crocodile from Gambia's head of state. Our present Queen, Elizabeth, received two jaguars (no, not the car) and two very large tortoises from the Seychelles. But the biggest animal presented to her was a seven-year-old elephant called Jumbo. The beast was a silver wedding anniversary present, but since it was too large to hang around the palace she donated it to a zoo.

For over 800 years the Kings and Queens of England have used the symbol of the lion to represent themselves and their country. Richard I started it all, and it has been used ever since. Great Britain's coat of arms has two supporters, which are the animals that stand on each side of the coat of arms: the lion that represents England and the unicorn, an imaginary animal with a horse's body, a lion's mane and twisted tail, and, of course, the twisted horn protruding from its head.

The early Scottish coat of arms had two unicorns as supporters. But owing to James I becoming King of England and Scotland, the two countries became united in 1707 and so one unicorn had to be dropped. Yet England still has three lions passent as its main royal coat of arms, which can be seen on the royal standard flag.

Did you know that in medieval days nighttime lighting was made possible by flambeaux? These were resin-soaked torches that were usually mounted in brackets on the walls. Candles made from animal fats were used as well. These tended to smoke and smell, but an even greater problem was keeping them away from the rats and mice that understandably loved to chew on them. The rodents were known to eat them even while they were lit. It is believed that this caused many house and other property fires. The candles were stored in a cradle made of tin to keep them out of reach of the animals. The best way to describe these candle canisters is to say that they looked a bit like a large rolling pin, and wire or string was put around each handle to suspend them from the ceiling so that nothing could get at them, except maybe the flies. Look out for these when visiting old buildings in England. One in particular that I know of hangs in the pantry of William Wordsworth's house in the Lake district. The canisters are very rare and are considered a collector's item.

Did you know that the royal coronation ceremony was actually started by King Edgar (Eadgar), one of our early Anglo-Saxon Kings? He organised an elaborate affair for his crowning, which took place on Whit Sunday May 11, 973, at Bath Abbey. The abbey was built in the year 676. It started off as the Convent of Holy Virgins, then in 758 became an abbey. Edgar was, in fact, the first and last King to be crowned at Bath by the Archbishop of Canterbury and York. But this very crowning set the standard for future coronations, and inside Bath Abbey you can see the Edgar stained glass window depicting this splendid ceremony. (Incidentally, King Edgar is buried at Glastonbury Abbey.)

The Romans built the first London Bridge, using wood for its construction and naming it Londinium Bridge. They placed it where they'd discovered the lowest part of the river and good grounding for the supports. The bridge greatly facilitated moving troops and supplies from the south. Yet the wooden bridge didn't last long, and one or two others preceded the stone one built during the reign of William I (the Conqueror). This bridge eventually became crammed with dwellings, as well as with stores that catered to first-time visitors to London from the south. It must have been quite a sight.

On St George's Day, April 23, 1390 (it was a Wednesday and it was raining), a most extraordinary challenge took place on this very bridge. It was, of all things, a joust held between Lord Wells of England and a hairy Scotsman called David de Lindsay. The idea behind it was to prove once and for all who was the bravest, most valiant knight. So with lances outstretched they approached each other at full gallop from opposite sides of the bridge. The hairy Scotsman won the third tilt. Yet as the English knight lay wounded on the ground, the victor, true to chivalry, ran to the side of his vanquished opponent and looked after him until a medicine man arrived. The Scotsman was at the bedside of the English knight every day until he'd fully recovered. They became lifelong friends and lived happily ever after. (Well, you have to have a good ending to some of the stories.)

Did you know that Queen Anne was Queen of Great Britain and Ireland, twelve American colonies, seven major Caribbean islands, Gibraltar, Minorca, Nova Scotia, and New Brunswick? Yet she had a terrible time trying to produce a few healthy children. Not only did she have several miscarriages, but she also gave birth to seventeen children, all of whom died either at birth or soon after. One did manage to survive until he was nine, then died when he became too excited at his own birthday party.

Incidentally, Queen Anne was plump, shy, short-sighted, and apparently very boring. She also suffered badly from gout and often couldn't walk. She was the only English monarch to be carried to her coronation in a chair. She died of a stroke on August 1, 1714.

Tobacco was introduced into England by Sir Walter Raleigh. He had the habit of smoking a pipe, which became very fashionable during the sixteenth century. One day, while smoking his pipe in a high-winged chair, his servant, unaware of this new smoking trend, threw a jug of water over him, thinking that his master was on fire.

While we're on the subject of smoking... did you know that King James I, although not very hygienic in his own manner, condemned smoking as a "filthy custom, loathsome to the eyes, hateful to the nose, harmful to the brain and dangerous to the lungs"? So there we are — our first official health warning way back in the early sixteenth century, and we still haven't heeded the message.

It is believed that Queen Elizabeth I had a crush on Sir Walter Raleigh, but she was a bit of a teaser toward the men in her life. You see, it's not the done thing for a person to ask a member of royalty the famous words, "Will you marry me?" No, the King — or the Queen in this case — has to do the asking and, well, she didn't. So Sir Walter hung out as long as he could, then finally got married in 1592 to another Elizabeth — Elizabeth Throgmorton, one of the Queen's ladies-in-waiting. (What on earth is a lady-in-waiting? What is she waiting for?) So when the Queen heard of the marriage, she was sick as a parrot and fell out with Sir Walter. That put her on the "I Hate Walt" list. Yet he managed to survive until King James I came along. Rightly or wrongly, Sir Walter was accused of conspiring against the King in 1603 and was eventually executed on October 29, 1618, at the Tower of London, where he'd been held prisoner. My belief is that the King of Spain put pressure on King James to have Sir Walter executed because he hated the man. Sir Walter had apparently made some rude remarks about the King of Spain. In fact, he'd said, "I would like to singe his beard." So Spain's ruler also got on the "I Hate Walt" list. After Sir Walter was executed for treason, his head was displayed at the entrance towers of London Bridge (the one that fell down). The story goes that his devoted wife paid some young chappie to climb up and get the head down (no jokes, please), and she carried it around with her until her dying days, twenty-five years later. Now, that's what I call devotion.

By the way, you can see the cell Sir Walter was in and the little walk area he had access to when you visit the famous Tower of London.

Did you know that Queen Elizabeth II was the one who gave permission to have her coronation televised live to the world — an act that made her very popular right from the start? Now, the day she agreed to have the ceremony, June 2, 1953, had been predicted by the country's top meteorologists to be warm and sunny. And guess what? It rained all day.

By the way, did you know that if you view the Queen's coronation you'll notice that the monarch holds a sceptre in her right hand and wears a glove only on her left? Wearing the glove is a very old custom that supposedly ensures that the future monarch will have a gentle touch with taxation. (What a waste of time. But at least we know where Michael Jackson got the idea of one gloved hand.)

Finally, while we're on the subject of Queen Elizabeth, did you know that she has two official religions? In England she's Anglican, and when in Scotland she's Presbyterian.

Did you know that King George VI's real name was Albert and he should have been crowned King Albert, but that Queen Victoria put a stop to that? She decreed that any future monarch with the name Albert should change his name to something different out of respect for her husband Prince Albert, who in 1861 died without notice of typhoid. (Anyway, how can you have a King of England with a name like Albert? It doesn't even sound like a King's name. Look at King Harold in 1066. That's why he didn't last long. He should have changed his name.)

King Richard III — it's a name that rings loudly in the history of England. There are those who support Richard and then others, like myself, who think he was a villainous creature, mainly because of the mysterious death of the two Princes in the Tower of London he was responsible for. Now, you might think I've been a bit harsh in stating this, but that's the way to look at early history. If something can't be proved, then you're entitled to your own opinion and you don't have to agree with what is written. This is a view held by many people. Richard III was betrayed at the climax of the Battle of Bosworth in 1485 by the Stanley brothers. When Richard and his army rode out of the city of Leicester to Bosworth Fields, they had to cross a bridge over the River Soar. The spur on his right leg scored a mark on the stone bridge that was spotted by a woman known to be a witch. She proclaimed that this was an omen and cried out, "On your return from battle, your head will hit the same spot where your spur did strike." In the battle, Richard was hideously wounded. His body was stripped naked, thrown into a horse-drawn cart and taken to the nearby town of Leicester. When the cart crossed the same bridge, Richard's head was dangling over the side and struck the exact spot as his spur had. The old witch was there to witness it, and a faint smile creased her face. He was buried without ceremony in an unmarked grave. His crown was found in a thorn bush. This is the reason many pubs in England are called The Rose & Crown.

Did you know that the early Crusaders had problems bringing the bodies of knights and other gallant people back to their own country for burial? They overcame this problem by boiling the dead body and bringing the bones back. In some cases they would bring the heart back too, and, having no ice chest, I bet it smelt a bit rank by the time they got home. (Maybe this is where the song "You gotta have heart" originated.)

Did you know that in the early days it was customary to lay the body of a deceased King or Queen on top of the coffin for all to see and, no doubt, to smell? Later, up until the early eighteenth century, it was the custom to have a life-size wax or a hand-carved wooden effigy of the person laid on top of the casket during its procession through the city for public viewing. (A death mask was especially certain to be made in order to prove the death of the individual.) Now, remember there was no refrigeration in those days. So you can imagine the state of some of the bodies that were buried.

If you visit Westminster Abbey, have a look at the few fine examples of the coffin effigies in the Undercroft Museum. Among them is King Edward III's, which was carved in wood. You can see that one side of his face was distorted from having suffered the severe stroke that killed him on June 21, 1377. And then there's Charles II's, Elizabeth I's, William's and Mary's, and Queen Anne's, as well as the effigies of others who weren't royalty, such as Lord Nelson. Although he's buried in St Paul's Cathedral, Nelson's effigy was placed in Westminster. This was done in hopes of attracting more people away from the newly constructed St Paul's, which was attracting people away from Westminster.

Did you know that Henry VIII's only son, Edward, who was crowned on February 19, 1547, reigned for only 6 years and 160 days? He was a short, skinny, sickly, frail chap, but very clever; if he had survived he would have made a great King of England. At the age of eight his father sent him to welcome the Admiral of France with two speeches, one in French and the other in Latin, both languages of which he could read fluently. Some early historians think that Edward was educated to death with all the long hours of constant studying. (So you can see why I didn't do all that well at school.) He was a very religious chap and was brought up to be Protestant, the new non-Catholic religion. He was very much influenced by people like John Knox, Crammer, and Ridley — all very active reformers. He also founded Christ's Hospital School, known as the "Bluecoat School." It was also during his reign that the prayer book was printed in English.

Edward also loved outdoor games; in fact, he would use any excuse he could to get outside. On many a day important visitors would arrive to have an audience with him, but he was outside having fun. During the year of 1552 his health started to decline. His doctors constantly bled him (one of the common cures of the day) and drugged him with all sorts of concoctions that only made him "worse-er-er." On July 6, 1553, while at Greenwich Palace, he finally died of tuberculosis.

Now, before his death he had commanded that both his half-sisters Mary and Elizabeth should be dropped from the succession, and he willed his gold hat to Lady Jane Grey. She was the daughter of the Protestant Duke of Northumberland and, in fact, the granddaughter of our old friend Henry VIII. (Are you still with me?) Well, you can imagine what had happened. The Duke of Northumberland had been Edward VI's protector ever since he was a young chap, standing in as a fatherly figure. Now, if you wanted your daughter to be Queen of England, you would wait until the present King was under the weather and would pop the question: "If anything should happen to you, my lord, God forbid, eh... why not instruct Lady Jane, who is a true Protestant, to take over the gold hat (the crown) instead of Mary or Elizabeth?" King Edward, sick as a parrot, tells him, "Yes. Yes. Now let me die in peace."

Because he knew he was dying and because of his great interest in religion he wrote this prayer: "O Lord, Thou knowest how happy it is for me to be with Thee. If for Thy chosen sake, send me life and health that I may serve Thee, O Lord. Bless Thy people and save Thine inheritance." Edward is buried at Westminster Abbey in Henry VII's chapel.

Many people when visiting England fall in love with the great thatched cottages that are scattered about the country. But did you know that the custom of covering the roof with this material goes right back to the Saxons? The word they used for anything that covered a roof was "thaec," and the person who put it on the roof was called a "theccan." Now, what did they put on their roofs way back then? The most common materials were vegetables and turf, bracken, heather, straw, and reed. It was a common sight to see vegetables growing on a roof year-round. Naturally, things got out of hand — heather and vegetables and grass growing wild. Finally, some smart aleck decided to clean up his house and just put straw all neatly running in the same direction with vines. Rocks were tied and thrown over the roof to keep the thatch in place. (This was a good move. It wasn't a pretty sight to see them try to get the lawn mower up on the roof.) So in the building trade things started changing for the better. Yet the word "thatch" still means "vegetable."

One of the major problems with thatch was the fire risk. You see, in those days chimneys hadn't been invented. Instead, imagine a fire in the middle of the room with the smoke rising up to the rafters and then filtering through an opening in the thatch. If a fire broke out in one house, it would invariably set the house next door on fire. Thus, a fire would simply spread from one house to another and sometimes wipe out an entire town. In the year 1212, it was made compulsory to give the thatch on a new roof a thick coat of whitewash to protect it from sparks. In the fifteenth century, thatch was wide-spread: even castles and many churches had thatch roofs. In fact, some churches still have thatch today. (In a village close to where I lived, the local fire station had a thatch roof. But it caught fire one day and that was that.)

To see a good example of a thatched house, have a look at Anne Hathaway's cottage at Stratford-on-Avon. The thatch is twenty inches thick and weighs over eleven and a half tons.

Did you know that in York one of the gatehouses is called Mickle-Gate-Bar, which is part of the great wall that surrounds and protects the city? This grand entrance is where members of royalty and dignitaries enter when visiting York.

In 1541 the gate, along with the entire city, was being decorated for a royal visit. Yes, our old friend Henry VIII was coming. In fact, a short distance away, in the north of the city, was a reminder of Henry's power: the ruins of St Mary's Abbey — just one of the many monasteries Henry had destroyed beyond repair.

It was also in York that the resistance, which was a sort of rebellion against the destruction of the abbey, had finally come to a head. The insurrection, called the Pilgrimage of Grace, was led in 1536 by a man named Robert Aske. He told his followers that he would like to go to London to deal with the so-called rule-makers. "God himself cries out against such evil," he said, "and

I know that I, with all my supporters, would like to go to London and have all the vile blood removed from the King's council." His attempt proved to be futile. Robert Aske was given a lot of empty promises; and as soon as his forces had disbanded, he and thousands of his followers were hanged for treason.

To encourage greater respect for his laws among his northern subjects, Henry established the Council of the North. This soon became one of the chief instruments for stamping out the Church of Rome in England. His most famous victim of that persecution was the wife of a butcher, whose shop can still be seen in one of York's famous streets, called The Shambles. In order to hear mass, Margaret Clitherow risked her life by opening her house to refugees and Jesuits. Her actions encouraged many Catholics to secretly worship in her house and in other houses in York. It wasn't long before word of this reached the Council of the North, and in 1586 this major crime brought her face to face with death. Knowing anything she said might bring others to the same fate, she chose silence. The result was, well, horrifying. The judge of the court announced: "You will be stripped naked and laid on the ground on your back, and as much weight as you are able to bear will be placed on your body. And on the third day you will be crushed to death."

While you're in the great city of York, when you visit the butcher's street called The Shambles, make your way to a road called Stonegate, which is actually built on top of a Roman road. There you'll see a famous figure called The Medieval Red Devil on the front of a building. This is, in fact, the old trademark of a printer. The story goes that it is a reminder of another revolution, but one in which no blood was shed. It is where John White had his printing shop in 1688. The Dutch prince, William of Orange, wrote a manifesto against England's Catholic King, James II. The majority of Englishmen wanted William to dethrone James, and the publication of the manifesto would be the first step. But all of the London printers considered it too risky to touch. Yet John White of York had the courage to print the document, and after the success of the great rebellion William rewarded White with the title of His Majesty's Printer for the City of York and Five Northern Counties. This was a wonderful boost to his printing business. It was White's wife who in 1739 started the first York newspaper, *The York Mercury.*

There's yet another street you need to visit. (Actually, you need to see them all.) It is York's smallest street, though it has the longest name: Whip-ma-whop-ma-gate. It means "neither one thing nor the other" and dates way back to the Saxons.

Finally, here's one more famous name connected with York. You'll see his invention at the York Museum. The fine horse-drawn hansom cab was invented by an architect named Joseph Alarwishus Hansom and became the country's first taxi cab. By 1834 his cabs were being talked about throughout the world.

When we talk about nursery rhymes, most people think about the words "lul"-a-"bye." These are old Saxon words that we still use. "Lul" means "sing" and "bye" means "sleep." And some nursery rhymes are actually sung, such as "Rock-a-bye baby on the tree tops, when the wind blows the cradle will rock, when the bow breaks the cradle will fall, down will come baby, cradle and all." In the early days many mothers used to hang their baby's cradle from the branch of a tree and allow the wind to rock the child to sleep. No doubt there were one or two branches that did break and tragedy struck. So by means of the song mothers were advised not to continue this method and to rock the baby in their arms instead — a tradition that we still practise.

Why do we always say the man in the moon — why not the woman in the moon? Well, the Saxons had a story about a man who was caught working on the Sabbath and was banished to the moon. And the full moon has always been associated with superstition. It could mean a good harvest, perhaps the birth of a child, or, as in the following, a declaration of a pure soul: "I see the moon, the moon sees me, God bless the moon, and God bless me."

Another Saxon superstition involved the rain. When the rain was unwelcome, it was the custom to send children out to curse it away. They recited a rhyme: "Rain rain go away, come back another day."

While we're talking about the moon, here's another one: "Jack and Jill went up the hill to fetch a pail of water, Jack fell down and broke his crown and Jill came tumbling after." This particular rhyme is closely related to the man in the moon story. And all of this is due to the story that parents told their children many years ago in Sweden. The tale goes that a brother and sister called Jack and Jill were fetching water from a well when they were captured and kidnapped by a man called Janny (the Scandinavian name for the man in the moon). He imprisoned them both on the moon, and it is the children that can be seen on the surface during a full moon as shadows. The words "Jack fell down" and "Jill came tumbling after" are seen as a reference to when the children (as shadows) disappear. The rhyme continues with the words "He went to bed to mend his head with vinegar and brown paper." This stems from a very early belief that those two ingredients would cure a headache. (How on earth you applied the two, I have no idea. Imagine coming home to your spouse saying, "Honey, I have a headache." and your spouse replies, "Oh, go and wrap your head in brown paper and vinegar.")

Did you know that the oldest pub in England is called The Ostrich and that it was built in 1106? Now, there are many pubs (the word "pub" comes from "public house") claiming to be the oldest, but they don't have any proof. Yet this particular pub can prove the date. The Ostrich stands near the end of a runway at Heathrow Airport at a place called Colnbrook. Like many other pubs, it has a dreadful history attached to it. Of course, the people who own it now are in good standing. But one pair of landlords in the seventeenth century, named John and Mary Jarman, were evil people. They perfected a way of murdering people who stayed overnight at the pub by using a bed. To explain... the room located above the kitchen was where they put wealthy-looking clients. Once such a client was fast asleep, John and Mary would creep into the room and pull a hidden lever, causing the bed to tip the person out onto a trap door. The door would open and the victim, falling into an enormous cauldron filled with boiling water, would be scalded to death. The deceased's belongings would then be stolen and the body disposed of. If anyone asked the whereabouts of that person, the Jarman couple simply said that their guest had left very early. Their last victim was a wealthy clothier named Thomas Cole. Suspicions were aroused when his horse was found wandering around the next morning, despite the landlords' declaration that Cole had left the pub. So after being interrogated (no doubt with a little brute force), Mary confessed. The clothier's body was located in the brook, and the Jarman couple were both hung. It turned out that Thomas Cole was their sixtieth victim. Incidentally, this is where the name of the little town, Colnbrook, comes from: Cole-in-Brooke.

While we're on the subject of pubs (and why not?), did you know that they go way back to the Romans some 1,800 years ago? You see, along all the great roads the Romans had carved out, there travelled huge armies, as well as those who supplied them. Now, where did these hordes of people stop for refreshments? Well, the Romans had this quite organised. Such travellers would frequently come across a wooden structure that sold wine and beer. And, yes, these Italians even came up with the first pub signs — although a bit primitive, but nevertheless pub signs. A bunch of grapevine leaves would be hung on a stick to indicate refreshments. As for beer, they stole an idea from the local people. Many of them brewed their own sort of beer, which consisted of fermenting apples and pears, various spices and herbs, and, of course, honey, resulting in a much sweeter beer than what we're accustomed to. In those very early days, if a household made a special brew of beer word got around, and the people living in the vicinity came to visit and offer an exchange of some sort for the beer. This would be known later as bartering. So the Romans would take the locals' recipes and use the beer to sell to their troops and higher-ranking officials. It was about this time that wine was introduced into England, and the Romans certainly knew how to produce that.

The Romans were in England for over 400 years. The next invaders to follow were the Vikings, and they certainly liked a beer or two. They brought their own brew over, something very similar to the local stuff. They called it "ole," which we locals, maybe after a few beers, changed to "ale." Later the Saxons came along and introduced their style of drinking. They liked the idea of everyone gathering in one room and getting roaring drunk. The name they gave to this place of entertainment was an "inn." Since the people of England liked the idea, these inns popped up everywhere, and it didn't take long before the country was flooded with them. So in the drinking world things started to get out of hand. Then in 957 A.D. King Edgar decreed that the number of inns should be reduced to one per village. He also initiated the standard drinking measure of a horn. (I wonder how that worked. Did you go into an inn and say, "A horn's worth of ale, please"? How big is a horn? There are so many different sizes, and if you were a Texan with a longhorn they would no doubt throw you out.)

Have you ever thought about the origin of "Eeny-meeny-miney-moe"? It's an early Saxon saying, and it's believed to have derived from the terminology used by the Druids' order as they counted out who would be their next victim for sacrifice, be it animal or human.

Did you know that the city of York is reputed to be the most haunted city in England? And without a doubt the most haunted building in York is the Treasurer's House. The site on which this building stands was once a Roman road. In fact, buildings of various shapes and sizes have stood on this very spot for over 2,000 years. Radulphus, the first Treasurer (or treasure keeper) of York Minster, was appointed around 1091 and took up residence in the building in 1100. But, sadly enough, the building, along with most of the city, was destroyed in 1137 during the Great Fire of York. Yet during the reign of King Edward I a new house was built that incorporated what had survived the conflagration. The prime reason for this building was to house the treasures of the Minister, since no other place existed in which to store such a large quantity of treasures securely and under one roof.

During the 800 years of its history, this building has been the home of a procession of interesting characters. So it's hardly surprising that succeeding generations have felt the presence of some of them still lingering in the building. The remarkable story of its Roman ghosts has made the Treasurer's House world-famous — and what a fascinating story it is! In the early 1950's during an archaeological survey, Harry Martindale, a young apprentice plumber, was working underneath the house (actually on the original foundations of what had been the cellars). He was in the process of knocking a hole in the wall for a heating pipe to go through. While working on the top of his ladder, he thought he heard the sound of a trumpet, and not very well played. At first he ignored it, but then the sound became increasingly louder, as though its source were getting closer. As the plumber was about to strike his hammer again, he caught a glimpse of the helmeted figure of a Roman soldier coming straight out of the wall, followed by a huge, lumbering horse with another soldier astride it. Harry Martindale fell from his ladder in amazement and cowed in the corner on the damp basement floor. Following the horse marched a line of what he called bedraggled-looking soldiers. Their shabby appearance and small stature surprised him. At this point he went up in search of his boss, who later said Martindale had appeared to be in a state of shock. The boss asked the apprentice if he'd seen a ghost, of course joking. After a cup of tea, Martindale was able to describe in detail the soldiers' appearance. Their spears and swords and round shields were unusually shaped for Roman soldiers, thus indicating that the kind of legion that had been in York was different from what was previously believed. The most impressive part of their outfits was the fine helmets adorned with plumes of feathers. For most of their short passage across the cellar floor, only the part of their bodies above the knees had been visible. Now, the interesting thing is that when these soldiers got to the area where the archaeologists had dug a hole to reveal the original Roman road, Martindale had seen the soldiers from head to toe and was able to describe the type of footwear they were wearing. Then when they got to the wall of the cellar they disappeared through that wall to the other side of the basement. Well, like all sightings of apparitions there is plenty of doubt. Yet when Harry Martindale was questioned by historians and other scholars, they were quite impressed by his accurate description of the soldiers, who turned out to be the Ninth Roman Legion. Not being interested in history, Harry's idea of what a Roman soldier should look like was what he had seen portrayed by Hollywood. But the chaps he saw were nothing like that.

One of the interesting elements of this story is that Martindale and many others working at the Treasurer's House were unaware of the other tales relating to Roman soldiers. At a fancy dress party given by Frank Green some time during the early nineteenth century, a young lady wandered into the cellars and had her way barred by a Roman soldier carrying a spear. When she returned to the party to ask the name of the ill-mannered guest in a Roman costume, she was told that no guest was so dressed! In 1950 a curator of the house saw Roman soldiers on horses when she went down to check on the boilers — again, in the basement. She has also seen the ghostly procession on a number of occasions, as have members of her family. From time to time visitors to the Treasurer's House tell stories of the phantom characters they've seen. So when you're visiting York, don't forget to pay a visit to this famous building.

By the way, in another cellar there's a tea room where you can get a nice cup of tea. You may well feast your eyes on these human vestiges of the ancient past. If one serves you tea, run like hell — it's a ghost.

Did you know that every year on April 23, St George's Day, a great ceremony takes place that is truly a sight to see? "What is it?" you might ask. Well, you know how we in England love to put on a pageant and carry on a great tradition. This particular bit of pomp and circumstance is the parade of the Order of the Garter. Let me explain: King Edward III was one of England's greatest soldier Kings. He would always be found at the head of the army, rather than hiding at the rear. And because of his involvement in battle, he had great support from his troops. He, in fact, captured about a third of France, so for a time a greater part of England's territory was across the Channel. (The French have never forgiven us for this.) Edward was a great lover of the Realms of King Arthur. He tried to replicate aspects of the knights in shining armour while he was King and would have loved to have been involved in that era. Anyway, the story goes that in the winter of 1347 he was at Windsor Castle feasting with all his noble knights. As usual, he was discussing the stories of his idol, King Arthur, and his knights were equally participating in the conversation. He had apparently always wanted to found a similar Knights of the Round Table. As part of the Christmas festivities he held a large ball, attended by anybody who was somebody. During the ball Edward danced with the beautiful Countess of Salisbury. When the dance was over the King bowed at the same time the Countess was bowing to him, and at this point the Countess's garter fell to the ground. Well, the King, being a gentleman, bent over, picked up the garter, and handed it to her. All around the King stood his trusted knights, who undoubtedly found this behaviour quite amusing and assumed that the King was having an affair with the Countess. But certainly not — the King was very happily married and didn't have an eye for the ladies. Yet the nobles, unaware of this, were muttering and sniggering, and things were generally getting out of hand. But the King put a stop to all this by saying loudly in a French Norman language, "Honi soit qui mal y pense," which means, "Shame on him who thinks evil of it." Words like this gained him tremendous applause from his close and faithful knights and friends. It was also an example of the customary comportmant of their King of Chivalry, Courage, Decorum, and Honesty. So this is, in fact, how the Order of the Garter got its name. There is a total of 169 Garter Knights — 13 times 13. (It's not known why that particular number.) You can't inherit this position; when a member dies the position is filled by someone appointed by Her Majesty, the Queen.

So for a colourful display of pageantry, try to witness this small part of English history. And arrive early to get a good view.

Did you know that in early Victorian days fashion for the ladies was quite uncomfortable? Take, for example, the corset. It was a work of art to narrow the waist, and getting dressed up took forever. Some of the corsets had whalebones as supports; others even had metal stays. Putting this item on sometimes required many hands. The really unfortunate woman had to lie on the floor face down so that a servant or friend could put a foot on her back and pull on the thick cord laces. A woman who had the money could purchase a winch (no, not wench) and get the thing really wound up tight, and — presto! — an instant figure. It was later realised that the tight corsets were responsible for restricting blood pressure and in some cases damaging internal organs. Even cracked ribs were reported. (And they wondered why ladies frequently passed out.)

While we're on the subject of fashion, what about the enormous hats women wore in those days? You literally had to keep a distance or else give the wearer a wide berth. And sitting behind one of these creations made it impossible to see past them. The unfortunate thing was that to keep it on her head, a woman had to use a very large pin that, when inserted, would go right through her hair. The trouble was that in high winds the pin would sometimes tear out the woman's hair when the hat was blown upwards. Yet, on the other hand, this was before the days of nerve gas and alarms. So a woman, if attacked, could remove the pin and, well, you get the point.

Did you know that there was no such thing as a family coat of arms? Now, there are a number of people who will disagree with me because many households are supporting one that they assume is of their family. Yet a coat of arms was presented to a person having a certain surname who applied for it — not to an entire family. It's not known when coats of arms first started, but we know that a certain form of identification was used as far back as the Crusades. This was called a surcoat, which was a long linen coat split at the side to allow movement, especially on horseback, as well as to protect the knight's armour from the heat and rain. The surcoat provided a means to display armorial devices. It was also known as a "coat armour," which was slipped over the suit of armour. Gentlemen of rank would have their coat of arms displayed on the front and rear of this surcoat — hence, the name "coats of arms." By the middle of the fourteenth century the surcoat had become much shorter and was known as a jupon. This was a sleeveless coat worn over the armour, very often displaying the wearer's arms.

The easiest way to understand the concept of coats of arms is to look in your pantry and take all the labels off the canned food, then shuffle them around and try to guess what's inside. So you see, a coat of arms was a form of identification. When knights were running around in all that armour, you wouldn't know who was canned up in there until you knocked him off his horse and found him flat on his back. Then you would lift the lid off and stand back in amazement when you saw that he was on your side. On the other hand, everyone knew who a labeled knight was.

Sometimes knights were seen with funny-looking objects sticking on top of their helmets. This was called a crest, and it was a secondary identification. If, for example, a whole bunch of knights were all in a group chatting away, you wouldn't be able to see the chaps in the middle, but you could identify them by their crest.

So coats of arms are not just pretty pictures. Rather, they are a part of history and mean something. And even if they're just one colour, that colour itself has meaning. Check into the coat of arms that has your name on it. You may be surprised to find a wealth of history about that picture that bears your name.

Did you know that in the very early days known as the Dark Ages, people didn't have second names? Instead, they were all known by their first name only. Imagine a small village tucked away in the woods, with everyone knowing not only each other's name but what each one did and who his or her parents were, and with most of the people bartering with each other for goods and services.

Well, this all changed when the country was taken over by the French — the French Normans, to be exact, in 1066. William I, known as the Conqueror, had no idea how big the country was or how many people lived in it. How was he going to rule the territory he'd acquired without knowing more about it? So he decided to call in the auditors to survey the entire area. He sent troops out to cover every square inch in order to record everything — every person, his sex and age, every building, every head of livestock, every acre of land. The troops were instructed to record anything that could be listed. Many people rebelled and tried to avoid giving information. Those who interfered with this effort were severely dealt with, and some even lost their lives. It was reported that young girls who gave their age as younger than it was were in some cases raped by the soldiers and then listed as women. So you see, it was quite a ruthless event. And once a person's name and property were recorded there was no appeal. This is why it was called the Domesday Book. The idea behind this monumental task was to impose a tax system so that William the Conqueror could pay the nobles who had helped him take the country and to pay for the great castles he built to defend what he had conquered. So this is the basis of the tax system in use today. (I suppose April 15 still carries the equivalent of that title: *Doomsday*.)

When visiting Salisbury Cathedral you'll see a very impressive tomb effigy of a knight of the Crusades in full armour, complete with shield and sword. Knights would be portrayed by adding colour to their effigy to make it look realistic; and a picture of this knight can be seen as it would have looked when first done in 1226. Yet this one looks unlike other medieval stone effigies because its colour has been remarkably retained. The name of this famous knight is Sir William Longespee, who was the Earl of Salisbury and a half-brother to King John. It was King John whose nobles persuaded him to seal the Magna Carta (Latin for "Great Charter") at Runnymede on June 15, 1215. Longespee was one of the witnesses to the sealing of the document. Now, most of this charter was for the barons' benefit. But of course a few things for the common people were thrown in as well. Anyway, out of eight copies of the charter only four survive today. And there would have only been three if it weren't for our Sir William Longespee.

The story goes that he received word that King John had ordered each copy of the Magna Carta to be burnt. So William put spurs to his horse and arrived at Salisbury Cathedral just in time. One of King John's men was setting his copy of the Magna Carta on fire, and William attacked him and knocked seven colours of dandruff out of him. He then quickly put out the flames and the copy was saved. Such is the reason this copy is burnt at the bottom. (Sounds like the ending of a good movie.) Of the four copies left, you may view one of them at Salisbury Cathedral by special request. Another is at Lincoln Cathedral, and the other two are in the British Library.

There are some loverly stories that go way back in history that would be quite difficult to validate. Yet having said that, most people like to hear a good tale, even though its ending may be sad. Well, here is one of them.

A sixteen-year-old lad by the name of Robert was known as the village idiot and only capable of ploughing the fields. On August 22, 1485, he was working with some of the other village lads when he suddenly looked up at the sky and shouted at the top of his lungs, "Now, now, Richard.... No, no.... Now, now, Henry, very badly done.... Richard, great!... Well done, Henry, well done.... Henry is the winner." You can imagine what the other chaps thought about him: "He's only got one oar in the water." The next day the news reached the village that at the very time Robert had been ranting on, the Battle of Bosworth Fields was taking place between — yes, you've guessed it — Richard III and Henry Tudor. It was a great victory for Henry. And it changed the tune of the local people about Robert. He was no longer the village idiot, but instead a kind of prophet. Not long after the battle dust had settled, Henry was given the gold hat (the crown, that is). He became known as Henry VII (and, later, father of Henry VIII). And would you believe that the King somehow heard about the young prophet named Robert and demanded that he come to London to visit him? Well, most people would be excited about such an invitation, but not he. Robert's friends told him what an honour it was to visit the King and that he wouldn't have to plough fields any more and that he would no doubt end up a rich man. But Robert was not too happy about it. He said, "The King will starve me to death." "Of course the King wouldn't do that," his companions replied. "He's fascinated by your skills." "No, no, no!" exclaimed Robert. "He'll starve me to death." And he simply did not want to leave the village. But the King commanded his presence. Robert reluctantly said his farewells to the village folk in a tone as if he would never see any of them again.

Before long he was standing in front of the King. Henry VII gave Robert a few tests to make sure he was not an impostor, all of which he passed with flying colours. The King rose to his feet and told the lad that he was an incredibly talented young man and that he could live there in his court. "You shall have anything you like and live in great comfort for the rest of your life. What have you got to say about that, young Robert?" The boy looked sick as a parrot and told the King that he knew he would be starved to death. The King burst out laughing and told Robert that this was one prophecy that would never come true. Then the King told his marshall to take the boy and feed him and treat him well. Robert was soon doing quite nicely, being supplied with wonderful living quarters, elegant clothes, and all he could eat. He was getting accustomed to this style of living. The only thing that didn't go down well was that some of the staff resented him, mainly because he had been a common plough boy at one time.

Some time later, King Henry had to leave London for a while, and he charged his marshall with taking care of Robert. And so the marshall did, until he too was summoned elsewhere. Well, he wasn't too keen on leaving the lad on his own because of the staff who would take advantage of him and perhaps bully him. So the marshall decided to put Robert in a room in the tower and lock the door to keep him safe. While he was away he completely forgot all about the boy, and when he was asked to stay longer he didn't refuse. The problem was that the marshall had the only key to Robert's room. When he finally returned he rushed to the tower and found that Robert had died of starvation, exactly as he had predicted.

Did you know that in Cambridge you'll find one of the four round churches that still exist in England? The church's official name is "The Church of the Holy Sepulchre," and it was built around 1130. These are the oldest remaining churches in England. They have the same construction as the round churches found in the Holy Land. And those were built by religious orders founded to guard the Holy Sepulchre at the time of the Crusades.

Did you know that King James I was brought up by a nurse with a drinking problem? So it was natural for him to adopt the same habit. He had difficulty holding his liquor. He drank a lot of beer, all the spirits he could, and gallons of wine. And, what's more, he got rid of it in the most filthy way, wherever he could and in front of whomever happened to be there. Most people, when they think of King James, credit him with the translation of the Bible, which not only was a landmark for religion in England but for the literary world in that it opened the door to publishing. Yet not many people know that James had a pamphlet printed about the disgusting habit of smoking and then levied a hefty tax on tobacco in an attempt to make people give it up. Since James was not exactly a role model for a healthy, clean-living person, it was surprising that he expressed such concern for the well-being of his people.

By the way, about the time the pamphlet was published another chap, the crazy Nicholas Culpeper, wrote a booklet called "Complete Herbal." He claimed that tobacco cleared the lungs, got rid of worms in the stomach, and cured headaches, indigestion, snakebite, and toothache. (This last one was accomplished by chewing the tobacco seeds.) Furthermore, tobacco ash could be used to clean the teeth, and tobacco juice could be rubbed on a child's head to kill hair lice.

One thing that King James was terrified of was witches. He also hated the sea. And he constantly wore a very thick padded jacket because he had this fear that someone was going to stab him. (Now, who would want to do a thing like that?) He committed many strange acts, but one stands out more than the others. Two brothers got into a fight and killed each other. (Since it's a long story, I won't go into that part.) King James said the two should not have died without a fair trial, so he put them on trial in Edinburgh and had the judge pronounce them both guilty. The Judge announced: "I find you two persons guilty and sentence you to be hanged by the neck until pronounced dead." The two dead bodies were taken out and hung again until they were dead... again. Well, you can't argue with a King, can you? James also had this notion that a King ruled the country under the direct command of God; thus, he thought he was above the law and could do whatever he wanted. This divine right of Kings, as it was classified, didn't do him one bit of good. Yet sadly this belief was passed on to his son, King Charles I. And we all know what happened to him.

When King James became very ill, his doctors prescribed large quantities of beer to bring his fever down. James couldn't resist that, and the beer eventually brought his fever down — in fact, right down. It killed him. He died on March 27, 1625, at the age of fifty-eight and was buried in Westminster Abbey.

King John. You know, the historians have painted this English King as bad King John. Even Hollywood did a good job of portraying John as a cruel, evil King. Now, there are many people in England, including myself, who would like to prove the early historians wrong. Maybe he wasn't a great King, but perhaps he wasn't as bad as he's been branded. Let me give you an example. His brother is celebrated by Hollywood as the great Richard the Lion Heart, a mighty warrior of the early Crusades. All right, he was a great fighter and is supposed to have slain a lion — of which we have no evidence. Yet he didn't succeed in any major victories in the Holy Land. And what he did succeed in doing was draining England's economy. These trips of his to fight the infidels were paid for by the taxpayers of old England. What with the cost of going on the Crusades and being held for ransom for the equivalent of three years' total revenue of England (which in today's figures is about two billion pounds), Richard was depleting the country's resources. And whose job was it to come up with this money for him? You've guessed it — Prince John. He had to get the money to pay for the King's ransom from the barons, who in turn hated John for dragging it out of them. And John had to take on this task so that England could get its King back.

Now, this great Lion Heart chap was King of England for ten years yet spent only ten months in his own country. He married Berengaria of Navarre on May 12, 1191, in Limassol, Cyprus. She never set foot in England. It was rumoured that the marriage was only a front for Richard's homosexuality. He had no children, except for several illegitimate sons. Berengaria died in 1230.

Later, during a battle in France, Richard got hit with an arrow in his shoulder — which he neglected, saying "I don't need any help." He kept on fighting and eventually died from the wound. The country's economy was at an all-time low when Prince John was given the gold hat to become King of England. First on the agenda was the monks getting together to meet with the new King. "Will you gather an army and go on a crusade?" was their first request. John stood up and shouted, "No! It is a waste of time and money that the country can't afford." The monks also stood up and demanded that he go on the crusade. When John again refused, they were furious and never forgave him. In fact, the monks detested John for not giving in to their request and hounded him for the rest of his life.

Now, what is important about this is that the monks were responsible for recording and writing the history of England. So bad King John didn't really hit it off well from the moment his reign began. And I suppose that if you're branded with this title of being bad... well, why not act the part? And he certainly did, for according to history he was not very popular. But again, what we read was what the monks wrote for posterity. (The same sort of thing happens today: if the press doesn't like you, you can be ruined. My belief is that this is what happened to John.)

King John also had a raw deal after he was dead. One day he and his army were crossing the Wash, which is a shallow part of the North Sea near Norfolk and can be crossed when the tide is out. The tide began to come in, sinking the King's carts and treasures, and even some of his troops. He went stomping off in a fury to the abbey at Swinstead, where the monks supplied him with peaches and wine and lampreys (a kind of small eel, which he loved). He broke into a fever from dysentery and, because he couldn't ride his horse back, had to be carried on a litter to Sleaford Castle. Since he was getting worse, he was then taken to the castle at Newark, where, after writing his will, he died at the age of fifty-three. I often wonder whether the monks had anything to do with his death. But we shall never know. He was buried at his own request at Worcester Cathedral in a prime place not too far from the altar. And guess what? Normally, when a medieval King died he was buried in full state honour with his royal robe laid across his body. Yet how was John-boy buried? Dressed like a monk. This was the monks' revenge on King John: lowering his powerful position in death to that of a common monastic.

But, wait — the plot thickens. John was at peace in death only until Henry VIII's brother, Prince Arthur, died in 1502. His father, Henry VII, and Prince Henry had King John's tomb moved from its original spot to a lower position and then placed Prince Arthur's elaborate tomb in John's spot. So even in death King John was put down.

You might have a different view of this subject, which is quite acceptable. But when dealing in early history don't necessarily accept the first story you read or are told. In many cases you can read between the lines — and listen between the lines as well.

The mother of our present Queen Elizabeth, known as the Queen Mother, was born in a haunted castle in Scotland called Glamis Castle. The Queen Mother has seen the ghost known as the Grey Lady. This apparition is of a women who was buried alive at Glamis Castle and is said to wander around the residence. Another ghost at the castle is that of Earl Beardie, who was quite a vicious chap in his time. He was very bad-tempered with his staff, and it's even reported that he drove some of his employees to commit suicide. There's also a female ghost running around who has no tongue. In life she had it cut out for being a constant gossip. (I wonder if she goes around trying to frighten people with sign language, and every time she swears she's told to wash her hands with soap and water.)

Farnham Castle in Surry is even more renowned because it appears to be the meeting place for royal ghosts. Elizabeth I wanders around there, as does her dad, Henry VIII, with the other daughter, Mary I. James I, George III, and even Queen Victoria have also been seen. Why they all congregate there nobody seems to know. What on earth do they talk about? So when you're visiting Farnham Castle, look out for these guests. Surely they must qualify for the honour of "by royal appointment."

Talking about the royals... what about King Charles I? (You know — the one who was directly under the control of God and not his Parliament.) Around the mid-seventeenth century, King Charles, who was in Oxford, decided to attack the town of Gloucester as part of the Civil War going on between him and Oliver Cromwell. But he discovered a problem: the town was virtually surrounded by water in the form of the River Severn. And being sort of clever he knew that the entrance to the town would be heavily protected. So he decided to outsmart the Roundhead troops, headed by a Colonel Massey, that were stationed in the town. King Charles sent for his top engineer and asked him to figure out a way to get his troops into Gloucester by a surprise attack. Well, his engineer, named Chilingworth, put on his thinking cap and came up with the idea of building a machine that would roll down the hill and flip open to span the river, thus giving Charles' chaps the advantage of surprise. He based his idea on a Roman machine that had been called the "tortoise." So the Royalists secretly started building this enormous machine, at times being scrutinized by King Charles when he visited. The King actually sat on a stone wall drinking his wine and no doubt having a picnic, watching the construction with great interest and occasionally telling the workers to get a move on. But, also in secret, on the other side of the river the Roundheads were able to observe what the Royalists were up to. So at night they dug away the banks of the river, widening its narrowest part.

The big day arrived, and King Charles was there to see the launch of this wonder machine. His troops all boarded this "tortoise" and got it rolling down the hill. It gathered speed, and as soon as it hit the water a mechanism was released that in turn released the expansion part that flung itself across the river. Yet instead of reaching the other side, the machine disastrously collapsed into the water, sinking almost immediately and killing many of the King's men. Oliver Cromwell's troops witnessed the event, and the only thing to be heard was the hilarious laughter echoing across the water. So Charles and his soldiers had to march off again in defeat.

Have you any idea which famous nursery rhyme refers to this disaster? Well, it goes like this:

"Humpty Dumpty sat on a wall,
Humpty Dumpty had a great fall.
All the King's horses and all the King's men
Couldn't put Humpty together again."

Did you know that in the early days traders who swindled their customers were severely punished? They would have to pay a heavy fine and often end up in the stocks for a day and a half. While they were on display, disgruntled customers could throw their bad produce at the trader and spew out all the verbal insults they could think of. In some places, such as Canterbury, you can still see the "ducking stool" that was used for the same purpose. In other towns the dishonest trader or shopkeeper would be dragged around on a horse-drawn sled with the bad produce hanging around his neck. If it were rotten fish that had been sold, well, I think the fellow would get the message to change his way of operating after that.

The bakers were always in trouble, so they introduced the system of giving their customers an extra roll or loaf of bread to allow for the odd one that wasn't fresh. This was called, of course, a "baker's dozen." In the thirteenth century the extra loaf was known as the "vantage loaf."

Another term from that period was the saying "to pay on the nail." This goes back to the traders who dealt directly with the farmers at market. A person selling something would put the goods on a large post that was stuck in the ground and had a flat top on it resembling a nail. Having put, say, a sample of grain on this flat top to show the quality, the customer, if satisfied, would put his money on top of the post to seal the deal. Thus, he "paid on the nail."

The Scottish "haggis" is a traditional Scottish dish, but not many people know that it was an English dish right up until the eighteenth century. (After that I think we decided to stick to our fish and chips.) Anyway, lots of people have tried haggis and have no idea what the ingredients are. Well, here goes. It's made from the heart, lungs, and liver of a sheep (some people use a calf) that are chopped up into suet, as well as oatmeal, onions, and seasonings all boiled in the sheep's stomach. (There were no Ziploc bags back then, and it had to be carried around in something.) Nowadays you can buy it in a can — yes, you can.

The haggis seems to taste much better on Robert Burns Night, held every year on January 25, the birthday of the Scottish poet. The poet's famous "Address to a Haggis" follows:

Fair fa' your honest, sonsie face,
Great chieftain o' the pudding-race
Aboon them a' ye tak your place,
Painch, tripe, or thairm: Weel are ye wordy o' a grace
As lang's my arm. ...
Auld Scotland wants nae skinking ware
That jaups in luggies;
But if ye wish her gratefu' prayer,
Gie her a haggis!

Now I bet you understood every word of that. This famous ceremony is a splendid sight. The haggis is laid on a silver tray and paraded into the room, escorted by a lone piper. Then it is placed on the head table and the poem is recited in true Scottish style.

During the reign of Queen Anne, who was crowned on April 23, 1702, people tried all sorts of things to get at her officials. Take, for example, her Lord Treasurer. He was sent a bandbox containing three pistols charged and cocked. The triggers had been tied with a thread and fastened to the lid so that when the unsuspecting person lifted it, the pistols would go off. When a chap by the name of Dean Swift was accepting the box, he happened to notice a suspicious string going into it. He quickly cut the string and thus saved the life of the Lord Treasurer. (Yes, even in those days there were creatures running around attempting to destroy people with homemade bombs.)

In medieval days, the English had their own ideas about crime and punishment. The most common crime was stealing. A person who was caught found himself in really big trouble. There was no police force such as we have today; instead, townspeople who were honest and law-abiding administered punishment. Someone caught stealing would have his hand cut off, and if the wound wasn't treated right the ex-thief would die of gangrene. An alternative punishment was to be branded just like a head of cattle. The X left by the red-hot iron on the former thief's forehead indicated to others that he was untrustworthy. Then there was the punishment known as disfigurement — in other words, nose-slitting. (Now that would make your butt come up to your elbows.)

In the town of Halifax, the Halifax Law stated that anyone stealing something whose value was more than thirteen and a half pence was to be executed on the Halifax gibbet, a kind of guillotine. In the Saxon days, a person who murdered someone, whether in a fair fight or in anger, had to pay a fine to the victim's family. Of course, the more important the victim the greater amount the perpetrator had to pay. If the result of a disagreement was a broken arm or leg, the same limb of the person who had done the damage was also broken.

So crime really didn't pay in those days. And the extremity of punishment certainly dissuaded people from committing crimes.

Did you know that in the days of chivalry it was a common sight to see a knight with a lady's glove tucked in his helmet, and that he would defend that glove with his life? In those times a folded glove was a sign of a pledge to fulfill a judgment by a court of law.

On ceremonial occasions one never wore gloves in the presence of royalty. This indicated that the person was not armed, and with the helmet and gauntlets also off it showed there was no hostile intent. Yet members of the clergy could wear gloves to indicate that their hands were clean and not ready to accept bribes. There's a story that Sir Thomas More, who was the Lord Chancellor, was given what was called glove money by one Elizabeth Croaker. She slipped him a pair of gloves lined with forty pounds when seeking a favour of him. Well, Sir Thomas kept the gloves but returned the money.

Gloves were also used to indicate a duel. This was accomplished by throwing a glove on the ground in front of whomever you were challenging. And the action of biting a glove was considered a pledge of deadly vengeance. (I've often wondered why my mother-in-law bites her gloves.)

We English seem to dwell on our country's legendary stories so much that many of us believe them to be true. Take, for example, the story of Lady Godiva. She was what was known as the Patroness of Coventry. (Coventry was a great medieval city; but during World War II Sir Winston Churchill allowed it to be bombed to the ground. And now it's a concrete city.) Anyway, Lady Godiva's husband Leofric, Earl of Mercia and Lord of Coventry, imposed certain restrictions and taxes that upset the locals, but that really infuriated his wife. She gave him some "stick" about how badly he was treating the poor. He told her he would reduce their taxes as soon as she rode naked through the town on a horse. It was a bit like our using an expression today such as "Sure, I'll do that when man starts to fly." Well, Lady Godiva did ride through town, and her husband did reduce taxes.

Like all legends, the story was embellished later on in history. It was claimed that in respect for the Lady, all the townspeople planned to shut themselves indoors at the time of her riding. Supposedly everyone did except for a certain tailor named Tom. He peeped through his window when she rode by and was struck blind because of it. The tailor became known as Peeping Tom, and eventually the term was applied to anyone who spied on others.

Every year since 1768 Coventry has re-enacted this legend: a woman with very long blond hair rides through the city on a horse with nothing on except her loverly long locks. There's also a full-size statue of Lady Godiva in the city centre. (You can't mistake the horse — he's the one with the grin on his face.)

Morris dancing is a very popular activity in England that originated around the fifteenth century. The dancers often represent characters from another legendary story — this one about Robin Hood. Other stock dancers represent Bavian the fool, Malkin the clown, a hobby horse, a dragon, and foreigners (probably Moors — also called Moriscos). The dancing was originally part of the May festivals, as was the Maypole and other pageants. All the dancers wore bells on various parts of their bodies. This entire act was brought over from Spain during the reign of Edward III, and it had previously been a military dance of the Moors — hence the name Morris dancing. The present-day chaps seem to have got the hang of this dancing. You frequently see them doing their thing in front of pubs. (No, I don't Morris dance. I tried tap dancing once, though, but gave it up when I kept falling in the sink.)

Do you ever follow a statement with the words "knock on wood" and then do just that? Have you ever wondered why we use that expression? Well, during medieval days people were very superstitious. When they had achieved something and hoped all was well, they commonly made a point of touching a tree — and not any tree. Only oak, ash, hazel, hawthorn, and willow trees had the power. Now, it was no good ripping off a branch and dragging it home for future use. It had to be a living tree that was touched. And if you didn't have one in your garden then you had to plant one. The Anglo-Saxons are who we have to thank for this superstition that has refused to die.

Talking about the Saxons... they were the ones who came up with the fortune rhyme that dates back to the tenth century. Reciting rhymes like this were how the common people passed down their earthly wisdom, usually in the form of superstition, to the next generation. They used to believe — and many still do even today — that the day a child was born would define his character for the rest of his life. You can still hear this rhyme in England.

> Monday's child is fair of face
> Tuesday's child is full of grace
> Wednesday's child is full of woe
> And Thursday's child has far to go
> Friday's child is loving and giving
> Saturday's child works hard for a living
> And the child that is born on the Sabbath day
> Is bonnie and blithe and good and gay.

So, on what day were you born? (By the way, in the olden days a gay chap was a bright, happy chap. So if you were born on the Sabbath, you're a fun person.)

Did you know that Edward I, who ruled from 1272 to 1307, was sitting in one of his Welsh castles playing a game of chess (for which he had a passion) and for some unknown reason simply got up from his chair and, as he was walking away, a massive stone from the rafters came crashing down and crushed the chair he'd been sitting in? Now, that's a checkmate, for certain.

King Edward's son, the Prince of Wales, was being knighted in 1306 at Caernarfon along with 300 other men, in a ceremony totally lacking in organisation. The noise and commotion were unbelievable. Things really got out of hand when everybody tried to get to the altar at once. Several knights fainted, many others were injured, and two actually died. The Bishop complained to the King, the result of which was a decree that this was never to happen again. Thus, bulk knighting was abolished.

Did you know that when there was a zoo at the Tower of London Henry I kept a polar bear and lions there? Visitors to the zoo would have to pay a fee, or else they could bring a cat or a dog to feed to the lions. (I wonder if those lions ever got fed up with the same old food — always cats and dogs. I can just imagine the beasts shaking their cage shouting, "Doesn't anybody have any chicken?")

Did you know that the flag of Great Britain is known as the Union Jack? It consists of three united crosses: the thick red cross of St George for England, the blue cross of St Andrew, called a saltire, for Scotland (added by James I), and the cross of St Patrick for Ireland (added in 1801 at the time of union). So this flag is technically described as follows: "The Union Flag shall be azure, the crosses saltire of St Andrew and St Patrick quarterly per saltire, counter-changed, argent and gules, the latter fimbriated of the second, surmounted by the cross of St George of the third fimbriated as the saltire."

Now, where "Jack" comes into this story, I'm still uncertain. I was always led to believe that the main mast on a ship was called a "jack," and that this was the mast from which the ship flew the flag of its country of origin. Later I read that a support for this very mast on which the flag was attached was called the "jack." Even later I read that the term for hoisting the flag was "jacking." So I really am not sure. Maybe the chap who hoisted the flag up was called Jack, and he had a patch over each eye and a smelly parrot going round calling people Jim Ladd.

Witchcraft. Often in the past even the sound of the word struck terror in people. Witches go way back to pagan and Celtic times. Because of all the stories and interpretations of who a witch was and what witches did, countless people have been executed when they happened to look like a witch or perhaps acted in a particular way. Or maybe only because they had a cat, or even a boil on their face. In England witchcraft became a felony in 1542; and by 1563 causing death by means of witchcraft was a capital offence. (And the death penalty was enforced.)

Witch hunting was the profession of a chap by the name of Matthew Hopkins. That is, he actually travelled around England looking for witches. He used several methods to determine whether a woman was indeed a witch. He knew that some concealed themselves in animals such as birds, cats, or toads. So if an individual were unfortunate enough to have one of these in her house or garden, then the finger was pointed at her. It was also known that witches fed their young on their own blood; so if someone informed Hopkins that a neighbour, say, were a witch, he would examine her body for what was known as "devil's marks," such as scars, birthmarks, or even insect bites. And there was no privacy when stripping these women while looking for such marks. If nothing could be found, the authorities did what was called "swum." The poor victim was tied up and thrown into a river or pond, and the verdict was guilty if she floated to the surface. Now, if she sank and drowned, well, she was innocent. Another method was to ask the woman to cry on command; if she couldn't shed any tears, she was declared a witch. The woman might also be asked to recite the Lord's Prayer; if she made even one mistake, "guilty" was the pronouncement. Another odd way to see if the accused was a witch was to get the large Bible from the church and weigh her against it. If she was heavier than the Bible, she was automatically guilty. Because of all this witch hunting, Matthew Hopkins and many more like him condemned thousands of innocent women to be hanged, burnt, drowned, or even beaten to death. Hopkins bragged about ridding the county of Essex of sixty witches in one year and of hanging nineteen women in one day.

But in 1647, after many complaints had been made against him, Hopkins was tested by his own methods. When he was cast into the river, guess what? He floated and was immediately hung as a witch. The last trial for witchcraft in England was in 1712.

Cooking up unusual dishes for royalty was always a challenge. The cook for King Charles I came up with an extraordinarily large pie, which of course was for entertainment purposes. When it fell to the Duke of Buckingham to entertain the King, he asked the cook to help him impress His Majesty by putting a little chap in the pie. Well, into this great pie he stuffed Jeffrey Hudson (1619–1682), a dwarf only eighteen inches tall. All went well, but the Queen, Henrietta Maria, wanted the little chap. He was duly presented to her, and she used him as a page. (No, not that sort of page. Maybe a bookmark.)

Much later, when Hudson reached the ripe old age of thirty and the height of three feet, six inches, he was made a captain of the horse regiment in the Civil War. He was later captured and imprisoned for supposed complicity in the Popish Plot. At one point the famous painter Van Dyck painted his portrait. When you're in the Tower of London, be sure to look for this little chap's suit of armour on display.

In medieval days it was quite common for a man to "strut" his wife up in a chastity girdle. This was to prevent her from being unfaithful while he was away. The problem arose during the Crusades. The knights and troops often fought on foreign soil for months or even years at a time. How was a woman to know whether her husband had been killed or lost? (Many Crusaders got either separated and lost, captured by the enemy, taken as slaves, or killed.) Just think how these women must have suffered, clamped up like that and with the hygiene involved in wearing such things. There were cases in which faithful ladies had waited years for their loved ones, but enough was enough. When they couldn't stand it any longer, they had the girdle cut off by some knight in shining armour. Then lo and behold their old man would come home looking for his faithful wife. Well, you can imagine what must have happened.

In museums in London and other major cities, you can see some of these chastity girdles or belts on display.

Did you know there's a big blackbird called a chough that's common in Cornwall and is even protected there? In fact, Cornwall has a chough on the crest of its coat of arms. The reason the bird is protected is that the soul of King Arthur was fabled to have transformed itself into one. Well, that beats the idea that he's sitting in a cave somewhere waiting for the perfect world so he can come and rule again. (What about this King Arthur? He succeeds in pulling the sword from the stone, then throws it into the lake. I'll have a lot to say about this chap later.)

Did you know that the familiar red- and white-striped barber's pole displayed outside the shop is a universal sign? The pole represents the staff that was gripped by a person undergoing venesection. It was painted partly in red since blood usually stained the staff, and partly in white to symbolize the bandages that were twisted around the arm prior to the bloodletting.

The word "barber" comes from the Latin "barba," meaning beard. The word indicates the profession of one who cut and trimmed beards, in other words, a hairdresser. Originally, barbers also practised dentistry and surgery. In the Middle Ages, the surgeons who pulled teeth used a pair of pliers or a clawed instrument called a "pelican." The patient was normally strapped to a chair or laid on the floor with his or her head between the dentist's legs. All teeth were extracted without any anaesthesia. It was recorded that some people actually committed suicide rather than suffer the agonies of the dentist. (Dentists are all right if they know their drill...)

The Company of Barbers-Surgeons in London was incorporated in 1461, then in 1540 it became the Company of Barbers and Surgeons, limited to drawing teeth. In 1745 it was renamed the Barbers' Company, which is still one of London's livery companies. Livery companies were and still are members of the City Craft Guild of London. Their purpose has always been to regulate pricing, quality of work, and wages, as well as to act as friendly societies (that is, charitable organisations). On special occasions they wear their distinctive livery, which indicates their trade — hence, the name livery company.

While we're talking about medicine... in the 1800's a doctor from Liverpool named Hugh Thomas pioneered a unique form of shock treatment for the sick. He would cure a slipped disc by creeping up behind the patient and giving him or her a sharp kick up the backside. Now, apparently this was quiet painful, but most of his patients were fixed. (You try that here and — instant lawsuit.) In his desire to work with the poor, Dr Thomas repeatedly refused promotions. When he eventually died in 1891 from long hours and hard work, over a thousand people attended his funeral.

On August 1, 1714, King William III was thrown from his horse while riding at Hampton Court when it stumbled on a molehill. The King broke his collarbone then later contracted pneumonia and succumbed a few days later. Well, when the news reached France, the exiled Jacobites, supporters of James III, raised their glasses and drank a toast: "to the little gentleman in velvet" — of course referring to the little mole that wears a furry jacket.

Poor Anne was William III's late wife's sister, who ascended to the throne on March 8, 1702. When I refer to her as poor Queen Anne, I'm thinking about the children she desperately wanted. Seventeen children she delivered, and only one lived beyond nursery age. All but one were stillborn or died soon after birth; the only survivor became too excited while celebrating his ninth birthday and died. They called the Queen Brandy Anne since she loved drinking the stuff. She also loved food and plenty of it; she suffered horribly from gout. It was so bad that she's the only monarch to have been carried into Westminster Abbey for her coronation. Another of her great loves was gambling.

Her husband, Prince George of Denmark, was as expansive as she was and just as dim. He spent most of his time working in his carpentry shop at Kensington Palace with a bottle of Scotch not far out of his reach. He suffered from asthma, and someone once said of him that "when he has a breathing attack and breathes very heavily, it's to indicate that he's still alive." Apparently, he didn't look much alive even when not suffering an attack. Many years later — well, more than a hundred — Queen Victoria made the remark that Prince George was "the very stupid and unimportant husband of Queen Anne."

As poor Queen Anne lay on her deathbed the doctors worked hard to save her, trying all the remedies they could think of — bloodletting, red-hot pokers that would blister her skin, various mixtures to make her vomit, even tying and wrapping garlic around her feet. Then some smart aleck came up with a brain-wave idea: he shaved all her hair off, leaving her looking like a snooker ball. But, sadly, nothing could be done. One doctor remarked at the death of the 350-pound Queen: "Sleep was never more welcome to a weary traveller than death was to her." She died at Kensington Palace on August 1, 1714, the last of the Stuart line.

By the way, it was during her reign in 1707 that the sealing of the Act of Union took place between England and Scotland, thus creating Great Britain.

Did you know that villages, towns, and cities are measured in miles from church to church? For example, if the signpost says sixteen miles from Hunstanton to King's

Lynn, the distance is measured from the main church in Hunstanton to the main church in King's Lynn.

Also, while we're on the subject of churches... in the seventeenth century the gentry of the towns and villages used to gamble large wagers on racing their horses from church to church. They could see the church steeple from miles away, and they would race as fast as they could in the most direct line while keeping an eye on that steeple. Whoever reached it first won the wager, or at least some of the money. This is where we get a term still used today in horse racing: steeplechasing.

One marvelous pub is The Smith's Arms, located in a small village called Godmanstone in Dorset. This pub is reputed to be the smallest pub in England. It has a thatch roof and is built of local flintstone, and it's so small it has humpbacked mice. The story goes that Charles II (1660–1685) was passing a blacksmith's shop and decided his horse needed new shoes. While the King waited for his assistants to take care of the matter, he asked the smithy to sell him a flagon of beer. Most blacksmiths brewed their own beer, and to cure it they put in a red-hot poker. They also used the poker during the winter to warm up the beer. (If you live in a freezing cold climate, you don't want a freezing cold beer.) Anyway, back to the story... the King answered the blacksmith by saying "I hereby grant you a license to sell beer. Now, for goodness' sake, sell me a flagon!" And the smithy did. And that blacksmith's shop has been a pub ever since. (By the way, in some pubs you can still see the old metal pokers on display.)

If you drive toward Sherborne when you leave The Smithy Arms (the name used by the locals for the same pub), you'll come across a very unusual 1,500-year-old carving of a figure in the chalk hillside, called the Giant of Cerne Abbas. This is a 180-foot long carving of a naked man with a very large club in his hand and his private parts in full view. Now, it was a firm belief that young ladies about to be married should sit on this giant in order to be fruitful in childbirth. This very old tradition possibly goes back to the early pagan fertility rights. These carvings have also been associated with the Celtic religious order. And still other people claim the Druids were the ones who left such marks around the country. The image is easy to spot: it's white and can be seen from afar.

When visiting the great city of Oxford, you'll discover that there are 653 buildings listed as being of "historic architectural merit." The first of my two favourites that I recommend you visit is the Shedonian Theatre. Up until the reign of Charles II, graduates of the University were awarded their degrees in the University church, called St Mary's. But for several years the church authorities had received notice that things were getting out of hand during the ceremony. Foul language and slanderous epithets were being shouted out. Of course, the authorities wanted to put a stop to that. Then a surprising supporter came to the assistance of the University by offering to finance a building especially for the awarding of degrees. The chap who came to the rescue was merry King Charles himself, along with his government. Now, since the church wanted this ceremony out of St Mary's, the Archbishop of Canterbury jumped up with a fistful of money and shouted, "Good idea. And I'll pay for it to be built." (Anything to get that rowdy lot out of the church.) So, that's basically how it started. Sir Christopher Wren designed the building, and it finally opened in 1669. It was named after the Archbishop, Gilbert Sheldon, and it has been the site of the degree ceremony ever since. No doubt the abusive language is still around. But when you keep in mind that the ceremony is carried out in Latin, I expect the abuse is a bit more palatable — or at least fewer people understand it.

Just opposite the Sheldonian Theatre is the other famous building, the Bodleian Library. This has been classified as the world's greatest library. The first University library was founded in 1320 and was expanded in 1426 by Humphrey, Duke of Gloucester and Henry VI's brother. By this time, the building was bursting at the seams with all the documents and early manuscripts it housed. Then came the Reformation, a religious and political movement in the sixteenth century. (It followed Charles II's head being chopped off by Oliver Cromwell on January 30, 1649.) During this period different religious orders destroyed manuscripts and books they didn't happen to agree with. The collection suffered an enormous loss.

But a gentleman by the name of Sir Thomas Bodley came along to save the day. He was, if you like, a book fanatic; his whole life was dedicated to books. He lived and slept them. So he founded the new University library using a tremendous amount of his own money. He also happened to be rubbing shoulders with the right person — King James I, who was also a book lover and scholar, and someone ready to give Bodley his full support. The King provided a few good ideas for the building's interior design. He also instructed the University to establish a policy "that under no circumstance was this to be a lending library; no book or document must leave the building." He also insisted that the librarian not be married (I have no idea why) and that no heating or lighting be installed in the building. Well, both of those conveniences were added much later. But the policy still holds that books cannot leave the premises.

Yet this policy wasn't always adhered to. King James' own son, who became King Charles I, visited the library during his reign and demanded to take a manuscript with him for further study. But he was reminded by the University officials that his father had instituted the rule that no book could be taken away. "But I am your King," he insisted. The officials were not amused by this and still refused to let him take the manuscript off the premises. He then said, "As your King, I demand to take this manuscript. And in return I shall grant your library anything within reason." Well, they just stood there with a big question mark over their heads and finally agreed to his request. The King then asked, "What would you like me to grant the library?" The officials' reply was "Just bring the manuscript back, please." No doubt the King left with a smirk on his face. So he was the only chap to break the rule. He was also the chap who thought he was above the law, and look what happened to him.

In front of the library is one of England's finest bronze statues. It's of the Earl of Pembroke, Chancellor of Oxford. On the wall is a statue of James I between two angles. How he qualified to get between two angles, I do not know. Well, I suppose he did organise the translation of the Bible, and he also declared that a copy of every book published in England, Scotland, and Ireland be sent to the Bodleian Library without charge. So you can imagine the number of books that have accumulated over the years. Not many people know that there's a series of tunnels full of books under the building, with a little railway and elevators in use to collect books.

Did you know that in 1194 there was a famous prince in Wales called Llywelyn ap Iorweth, Prince of Gwynedd? ("Ap" in front of a Welsh name means "son of," just as "Mac" does.) There's a legendary story about this chap that goes something like this... One day Prince Llywelyn decided to go out hunting, and instead of taking his favourite hunting dog named Gellet, he instructed the animal to stay in the nursery to look after his one-month-old baby son and heir. Then off he went with his other dogs. Well, after a long day at the hunt, the Prince, quite exhausted, made his way back to his palace with the deer and other wildlife he had killed. As he neared his abode at the foot of Snowdonia Mountain, his hound Gellet came bounding out to greet him, barking and wagging that great tail of his. But as the dog got closer, the Prince was puzzled to see that Gellet's face and jaws were dripping with blood. His thoughts suddenly flashed to his baby son, and he put his spurs to his horse and raced into the palace, up the stairs, and finally into the nursery. The room was in turmoil — everything turned upside down, blood splattered all over the walls and floor, but no sign of his baby. Prince Llywelyn's eyes filled with tears and his heart filled with sorrow. He stared up at the ceiling crying, "No, no!" Then, looking down at his favourite dog, who was sitting at his side looking up at his master with his tail wagging, the Prince cried to the hound, "How could you do this?" He drew his sword, thinking only of his son, and plunged the blade into the dog's throat. At that moment, as he endured the agonizing sounds of Gellet dying, he suddenly heard the faint cry of a baby coming from beneath the upturned haycase (or mattress). Throwing his sword down, he lifted up the haycase to find his baby, safe and well, lying beside the body of a wolf that Gellet had killed.

The Prince was later found lying on the floor with his baby in one arm and his other arm around Gellet. It was reported that he cried for a fortnight and a day and was never seen to be happy again during the rest of his life.

In medieval days most towns had a church, and the church usually ran the annual fair. (The word "fair" is based on a Latin word that simply means "holiday.") Since the church controlled everything else in the townspeople's lives, it was only logical that it would also control their holidays. The fair consisted of side shows, amusements, food vendors, and the like. Plenty of jolly good old English fun. Now, just like the travelling players, you had what is known as the travelling fairs. Sometimes the fairs would conflict with the players, and that made it even better.

Some of the most famous fairs were the Goose Fair (still held every year in November at Nottingham), the Paddington Fair (in fact, a public execution fair at Tyburn, which is in the Paddington area of London), and the famous Scarborough Fair in Yorkshire, to name but a few.

Another popular fair was called the Mop Fair. To explain... its original purpose was a hiring fair — a sort of travelling employment event. People who were looking for work would arrive dressed according to their trade, or else carrying their trade tools. For example, a ploughman would wear a smock with a picture of a plough on it; a shepherd would carry some wool and a crook; a maid would wear a maid's outfit; and a cleaner would carry a mop. Since there were more cleaners than any other trade, thus, the name of the fair. After the fair had moved on, about a week later it returned for one day and was known this time as the Runaway Mop Fair. Its purpose was to give participants a chance to change their minds about either their job or their employer, and vice versa. The two fairs continue to take place even today, although the context is different. Nowadays proceeds from the fairs go to various charities.

Talking about churches... if you look at some of the oldest of them you may well see at their outside entrance a lych gate. This is a roofed gateway, either large or small, and sometimes thatched. Yet all of them served the same purpose: they were built as a place to keep a coffin before it had been accepted for burial in the holy ground of the church. You see, in the early days proof had to be provided that whoever was in the coffin was a Christian and worthy of being buried in consecrated soil. If the deceased had been hung or had taken his own life, he couldn't be given a Christian burial. So the priest would meet the deceased's survivors at the lych gate and examine the contents of the coffin. And since it's always raining in England, it was a considerate gesture that a shelter had been built to wait under.

In 1770 the Lord Mayor of London was a man named Brass Crosby. Around this time the publication of Parliamentary proceedings was still forbidden by law. But Mayor Crosby, as chief magistrate, released documents to the printers of the *London Evening Post*. (For what reason it's not sure.) For his wrongdoing Crosby was committed to the Tower of London. Yet since he was a popular chap as well as the mayor, the people rallied to his support and thus secured his early release. His boldness to do such an act developed into a saying that used his name: "bold as brass."

While on the subject of Lord Mayors... another famous name comes to mind: Richard (Dick) Whittington, Mayor of London on three occasions, 1397–1398, 1406–1407, and 1419–1420. He was a gentleman of great wealth who actually gave personal loans to three Kings, Richard II, Henry IV, and Henry V. His wealth came mainly from coal, which was brought into London by large "cats," a sort of barge that travelled on the River Thames. Dick Whittington has always been associated with the Christmas pantomime, a theatrical entertainment based loosely on old nursery rhymes or fairy tales. The Dick Whittington pantomime always involves his cat. How that element got into the story is not clear. It might even be a pun on the word used for his coal-carrying barges.

Have you ever thought where the months of the year get their names from? Well, let's have a look at January. This, of course, comes from a Roman chap called Janus. He was the ancient Roman deity who kept the gates of Heaven. Hence, he was known as the guardian of gates and doors. He apparently had two faces. (No mother-in-law jokes, please.) So he could look back on the past year and also look forward to the current year. The Saxons used to call this month Wulf-Maand, which meant "frosty month." (And if you've ever been in England during February, you'll know that the frosty bit is right.)

Did you know that on February 12, 1429 (during the famous Hundred Years' War), Sir John Falstaff was taking supplies to English troops who were being besieged at Orleans, when suddenly he was attacked by the French? (Yes, they were at it again.) Since his wagons were not set up with enough weapons, he resorted to opening some of the barrels of supplies. Well, the barrels he opened happened to be full of salted herrings. He and his men took sheer delight in throwing tons of stinking herrings at the enemy, and the French, unable to stand it, actually fled. (If it had been frogs being thrown at them, it might have been different.) This battle was known in English history as the Battle of the Herrings.

There's a famous part of London that is regaining its rightful fame. It's called Southwark (which means "southern fort") and it sits on the banks of the River Thames on the south side of the city, just opposite St Paul's Cathedral. This part of London was first established in 1327 and was known as "The Borough." A great deal of history is associated with it, including the site of the Tabard Inn mentioned in Chaucer's *Canterbury Tales*, the George Inn, the Clink (the name of a well-known jail that was later used to refer to any jail), and Paris Gardens — and don't forget St Mary's. But what is making Southwark famous again is the rebuilding of the Globe, which, as you know, was Bill's "wooden O." The construction of the new theatre near the original sight was instigated by the American actor Sam Wanermaker, who unfortunately died before he could see his project come true. So when you're in London, go see this great new "wooden O." You'll be amazed at this wonderful dream that has finally come true.

In English history there have been many, many murders that have yet to be solved, and the chances of solving them are very remote. Take, for example, the famous Tower of London. All sorts of nasty business has gone on in there — and what better place? So few witnesses, and so many strong closed doors. If somebody were to scream or to shout for help, one would just assume that the poor wretch was being questioned or tortured and think nothing more of it.

Two of the most famous deaths in the Tower were those of the two Princes, Edward V and his brother Richard, Duke of York. You see, Edward succeeded to the throne on April 9, 1483. At the time he hadn't been crowned; but waiting in the wings was his officially appointed guardian, his uncle Richard, Duke of Gloucester. Now, Richard feared the power of the Woodvilles,

Edward's family, so he arrested their leaders and killed Edward's grandfather, Earl Rivers, and an uncle, Lord Hastings. Richard had sent for Hastings to appear before him at the Tower of London, where he falsely accused him of treason and found him guilty. Richard shouted, true to his nature, "I will not eat supper tonight until Hastings' head is removed!" Hastings was immediately escorted down the stairs and thrown across a nearby tree trunk to have his head chopped off. (This is history repeating itself: as one person assumed the throne, it was customary to eliminate anyone who posed a threat. So relatives were inevitably thinned out in the process.) Next, Richard forced Edward's mother, Queen Elizabeth, to seek safety in Westminster Abbey. (Well, he didn't want to kill too many royals.... It might look bad.) Then he started spreading rumours that both of the young Princes were illegitimate, using the pretext that Edward IV's marriage was invalid. He managed to bully Parliament into agreeing with him. On the day set for young Edward's coronation it was proclaimed that the Duke of Gloucester should now be called King Richard III. He'd done it. He'd actually pulled it off. He was now King of England, and with it came not only a gold hat but power. With this great position he could, in fact, do whatever he wanted, or else get people to carry out his commands.

Now, what about the two young Princes in the Tower? As long as they were alive, they were a threat. You can imagine this little "humpty" King (Richard was nicknamed "humpty" because of his humpback) going to the Tower, sliding up to a couple of guards on duty, and slipping a few gold coins into their palms, saying, "There's a little job I want you to take care of. You know the two young chaps in the royal chambers? Well, get rid of them and leave not a trace. Tonight!" In 1674 workmen were repairing the stairs in the white tower when they came across the skeletons of two children. The remains were given a decent burial amongst Kings at Westminster Abbey in an urn designed by Sir Christopher Wren.

This is a classic unsolved mystery. Many people claim that Richard didn't do it, but as far as I'm concerned, the finger points at him. And what happened to Richard? Well, he only lasted two years and fifty-seven days. Then he was brutally murdered at the Battle of Bosworth Fields on August 22, 1485. His body, stripped naked, was thrown in a horse-drawn cart and unceremoniously taken to the city of Leicester. He was buried in an unmarked grave at Greyfriar's Chapel. This shows you what the people of England thought about the chap.

Someone else who "accidentally" died was the brother of the King before Richard, that is, Edward IV's brother, George, Duke of Clarence. He had apparently supported the wrong chap, the Earl of Warwick (known in history as the Kingmaker), and so his brother, being very cautious, had him locked up in the Tower. Now, it would seem that once a person was in there he'd no longer be a threat. Right? Wrong in the event that he escaped. So George had to be gotten rid of, although it was made to look like an accident. (No doubt these guards also had their palms crossed with silver or gold.) The official story was that he got drunk and fell into a vat of malmsey wine.

Then there was the Duke of Northumberland, who, during the reign of Elizabeth I, was sent to the Tower on suspicion of treason, which he strongly denied. Anyway, one morning the guards (again, no doubt, with a great number of coins in their pockets) declared that to their surprise they'd discovered that the Duke had committed suicide. (Right — he was lying on his bed in his cell, having been shot with a pistol and stabbed to death with a knife.) Again, another case of unsolved crimes.

Incidentally, in 1606 the Duke of Northumberland's son was also sent to the Tower, but he moved in his extensive furnishings and enjoyed all the comforts of home. He entertained friends there and was generally having a great time. Twenty-five years later, in 1631, they told him that he was free to leave, but he didn't want to. He was onto a good thing — everything being taken care of — and now they wanted to throw him out of the Tower. The warden had to beg him to leave, saying "But we need your cell." The Duke eventually gave up and left. (You wouldn't have seen my feet for dust, if that were me.)

While we're talking about the Tower... there have been some successful escapes and some not so successful. Take, for instance, the Welsh prince, Gruffudd Ap Llywelyn. In 1244 he had a large rope smuggled into him, then he threw it out the window and climbed down it. But it was far too short, and as there was no turning back, he fell and broke his neck. In 1649 Lord Capal managed to get out of the Tower and, as he was very tall, waded across the moat. (In those days the

Tower was surrounded by a moat; nowadays it's all lawn.) In 1320 the Earl of March slipped into the kitchen, climbed up its chimney, then jumped across rooftops and crossed the moat at low tide. Then there was the Earl of Nisdale, who had some women's clothes brought in by his wife and walked out of the Tower the day before his execution dressed like a maid. (You see, it pays to dress in women's clothes.) A friend of the Duke of Monmouth, Lord Grey, was being escorted to the Tower, and on the way gave his escorts some wine to drink. As it was cold, they enjoyed more than a little. And by the time they got to the Tower, where a large crowd was waiting, each and every one was roaring drunk. The escorts marched into the Tower without noticing that Lord Grey had slipped away. He managed to flag down a boat for a ride to freedom.

The only prisoners at the Tower today are the ravens, birds of ill omen, fabled to forebode death and to bring infection and bad luck. King James ordered the birds removed from the Tower, but it was pointed out that because of the superstition surrounding them it would be wise to keep the ravens and make sure they stayed. The belief was that should the birds leave the Tower, not only would it collapse but the monarchy would also fall. Because of this, six ravens have always been kept prisoner in the Tower. There is even an appointed keeper of the ravens to ensure that nothing becomes of them. Should one die, it has a special burial place known as the Ravens' Cemetery. (It seems such a waste burying those big fat birds since they taste like chicken.) When a bird has to be replaced, a trip to Cornwall is made, since that is where they can be found in abundance.

Attempts were made to breed the ravens at the Tower. Some type of raven specialist selected a male and female and allowed their wings to grow, since when they mate they have to fly high and do that spiral display before they can actually... well, do it. The male bird flew high and, having heard all about prisoners at the Tower, flew away. The female stayed but was attacked by the others, perhaps jealous because she could fly. Anyway, that's why the birds aren't bred there. See how many you can find when visiting the Tower of London.

Drinking tea in England is not only a pleasant pastime but part of our tradition. If things aren't going too well, simply put on the kettle and make a nice pot of tea, and things will sort themselves out in no time.

Way back in the 1600's a chap by the name of Thomas Garway was in fact advertising tea as a tonic good for curing headaches, stones, loss of sleep, loss of memory, scurvy, gravel, and dropsy. (Well, that's one way of getting people to drink the stuff.) Even Queen Elizabeth I thought it was a good idea to promote tea for profit through the newly formed East India Company. Tea was actually a very important source of revenue for the British Colonial Empire for 250 years. In the seventeenth century King Charles II was obsessed by the drink and collected anything that had to do it.

It was the Duchess of Bedford who came up with the idea of "afternoon tea." Her husband was out hunting and was much later than usual in returning. So the Duchess had the tea served with pastries and cakes, thus taking care of her guests' hunger until time for dinner.

Did you know that at the World's Fair at St Louis in 1904 the East India Company set up an exhibit to promote their tea? Yet since it was quite hot few people wanted a steaming cup of tea. So the supervisor, a chap by the name of Richard Blechynden, put lots of ice into the tea urns, and people were soon standing in line wanting to sample the beverage. That was the introduction of iced tea in America.

Not many people know that in 1912 another chap from England named Thomas Sullivan was trying to get some retailers interested in his tea by sending them samples of different blends. He sent the samples in little hand-sewn silk bags. Well, the idea was soon taking on, and Sulllivan's customers were asking for more samples. So he sent them more, but not in silk bags. Instead, he used a substitute gauze bag, thus inventing the now common tea bag.

Incidentally, opinions vary as to whether you should first pour the milk or the tea into the cup. Well, here's the answer. In the early days of China, where the populace was drinking tea before we English did, the custom was to add the milk first, if it was being used. The reason was that the cups, made of such delicate thin china, which would crack if the boiling hot tea were put in first. So I hope I've sorted that out once and for all.

So when in London, may I suggest you have an afternoon tea in the best possible way? Visit the Ritz Hotel, Piccadilly, London. (And don't forget to stick out your little finger when holding your cup.) It will be expensive, and you may have to book ahead. But it's a tea served the correct way that you'll never forget.

We already had a go at King Henry II. Remember that he was the one who ordered the murder of his once good friend, Thomas Becket. Well, did you know that he came to the throne via his mother, Matilda? (Her sister with the same name went waltzing off to Australia.) But it was his father, Geoffrey, Count of Anjou, who provided the new dynasty its name. Geoffrey went by his nickname "Plantagenet," given to him because he always wore the flower from the broom plant whose Latin name was *planta genista*. Well, it seemed that most people liked the name, so the entire family was known as the Plantagenets. Now, this has nothing to do with what I'm leading up to. But I thought I would let you know just in case you were wondering.

Right.... Henry II was a tall, handsome chap, strong as a lion, quiet and intelligent, but he was forceful and had a terrible temper that got him into more than enough trouble. And talking about trouble — his wife, Eleanor of Aquitaine, was a pain. They were always fighting with each other, but in between fights they managed to produce five sons and three daughters. (No TV in those days, you know.) She was much older; when they married he was nineteen and she was thirty. Anyway, the story goes that Henry had a very attractive young lady on the side and was frequently seeing her in secret. In fact, he built her a nice little cottage tucked away from prying eyes (especially from those medieval paparazzi) right in the middle of a garden that resembled a maze. When Eleanor heard about the affair, she was sick as a parrot. Wanting to find out where the paramour lived, unbeknownst to the King she cleverly tied a long thread of cotton to his cloak. Well, His Majesty set off, telling Eleanor he was going for a quiet stroll and wasn't to be disturbed. "Yeah, right," thought the Queen, and later set off to follow the long line of cotton. She eventually arrived at the little cottage and found her husband embracing the beautiful young lady known as "the fair Rosamond." Now it was the King's turn to be sick as a parrot, and after a few words he stormed off. Queen Eleanor confronted the woman, saying, "Look, I have in my left hand an attractive dagger that I expect you to plunge into your heart. Or, in my right hand I have a small attractive bottle of poison. Which shall it be?" It didn't take long for the fair Rosamond to reach for the small bottle. Eleanor watched her drink the contents, then watched her keel over with her feet in the air. All this took place in 1177 in what is now Blenheim Park at Woodstock. Rosamond was buried at Godstow Abbey, Oxford, with a verse carved upon her tomb in Latin whose translation is

> "Here Rose the graced, not Rose the chaste, reposes;
> The smell that rises is no smell of roses."

You can see that the monarchs of England were at it even in those days. So what we hear today about the royals is nothing new. It's simply another case of history repeating itself.

Have you any idea what the word "resurrectionists" means? Well, in simple terms it means "body snatchers." These were people who broke open freshly buried coffins and stole the bodies to take to medical schools for surgical study.

The first record of this crime goes back to 1742. Then in 1832 a law was passed that made it a misdemeanour to take a body to sell, and a felony if the body were clothed.

Two Irishmen in Edinburgh, William Hare and William Burke, had a nasty little business going of supplying bodies to a surgeon named Dr Robert Knox. When they couldn't get the bodies from the graves because the graveyards were too closely guarded, they turned to the pubs. After spotting a candidate the two would get the person drunk and take him or her home. They would smother the sleeping victim then deliver the body for cash. Incidentally, a man's body brought ten pounds and a woman's five pounds. (No, please don't ask.) The two Irishmen got away with this crime fifteen times before being caught. Burke was hung for this terrible crime, but Hare turned King's evidence and, under Scottish law, was a free man. (This is where the term "scot-free" comes from.)

Are you familiar with this verse?

"Little Miss Muffet sat on a tuffet
Eating her curds and whey
Along came a spider and sat down beside her
And frightened Miss Muffet away."

The origin of this nursery rhyme is related to an entomologist named Dr Thomas Muffet. (In Texas they're simply called "bugologists.") One day he and his daughter were out in the country having a picnic, no doubt surrounded by tuffets (clumps of grass), when a large garden spider happened to come and see what was going on. This frightened poor Miss Muffet away. Thus, the origin of the nursery rhyme children still recite today.

Carisbrooke Castle is a splendid castle to visit, situated on the Isle of Wight off the southern coast of England. There was a fortification of some sort on this site long before the castle you see today, which goes back to the twelfth century. The interesting story related to the castle concerns King Charles I, who was hiding from Oliver Cromwell's lot. He had just escaped from Hampton Court, where he was being held prisoner. And since the Isle of Wight was part of his kingdom, he thought he would seek support from the Governor, Colonel Hammond, who was also the brother of the King's chaplain. But the Governor supported Parliament, who in turn supported Cromwell. What do you do when your King comes asking for help and you know he's on the run from his country? You lock him up, of course. Well, basically, that's what happened. Yet he was treated with dignity, being wined and dined and given anything he wanted except for hacksaws and rope ladders and the like. Life wasn't too bad for the King. He went horseback riding with Colonel Hammond, and he even had a bowling green made for his pleasure. If the King happened to ask for too much, he would be reminded that he was a prisoner and not a guest.

On March 20, 1648, King Charles very nearly escaped. He was being held in the constable's lodgings that adjoined the great hall. It had been arranged that he should escape at night through the window, lower himself down with a cord that had been smuggled into his room, and run across the courtyard to the easily scalable curtained wall behind the Chapel of St Nicholas. On the other side of the wall two of the King's men would be waiting with a spare horse. Well, things might have gone as planned, but unfortunately it didn't occur to the King to make sure he could get through the window. He'd put on so much weight that he got wedged in it. The guard outside the King's room had his curiosity aroused when he heard grunting sounds, so he went in and helped the King get back in again.

On May 28 Charles made another attempt to escape, after he'd been moved to another room whose windows were barred. Now, somehow the King had been supplied with a large quantity of nitric acid with which to cut through the bars. It's much quieter than a sawblade. The problem this time was that far too many people were in on the escape, and it wasn't long before word got to the Colonel. He burst into Charles's room and said, "I am come to take leave of Your Majesty, for I hear you are going away." The King stayed in that room under heavy guard until he was removed to Newport on September 6, 1648. And, as you know, on January 30, 1649, at 11 o'clock in the morning Charles was executed.

Do you remember that in Shakespeare's *Macbeth* the second witch says, "By the pricking of my thumbs/Something wicked this way comes."? Well, once again we have the ancient Romans to thank for the superstitious belief the witch was expressing. The Romans believed in and took quite seriously many superstitions. Here are a few examples. When your ears tingle, it means someone is talking about you. When a sudden fit of shivering occurs, it's because someone is treading over the place that eventually will be your grave. When your eye twitches, this indicates an upcoming visit from a friend. When the palm of your hand itches, it shows that you're going to receive a present. If your bones ache, stormy weather is coming. And a sudden pricking pain is a warning that evil lurks ahead. These are only a few of the superstitions that continued to circulate in England even after the Romans were gone. Some people still strongly believe in them and will go out of their way to avoid walking under a ladder, crossing a stranger while climbing stairs, or cutting their toenails on Sunday. No doubt you know many others. Yet nearly all of them go back to the Romans.

By the way, men in the Roman army were issued tablets of salt, which in those days was very valuable and necessary. These chaps became known as the "salters." Over the years the word was gradually corrupted from "salters" to "soldiers."

Henry VIII's first wife was Catherine of Aragon. Yet earlier she had been betrothed to Prince Arthur, Henry's brother, who was preparing to become the next King of England. Catherine and Arthur got married in 1501, but tragedy struck when the Prince suddenly died. Henry was next in line to be King. He also had a crush on Catherine. When she was subsequently betrothed to Henry, he was now clicking his heels. Not only had he obtained the gold hat, but a beautiful woman to be his Queen as well. He ascended to the throne on April 22, 1509, married Catherine on June 11, and was crowned on June 15. And for almost twenty years they were known as the perfect royal couple... well, apart from his affairs with Elizabeth Blount, who bore him a son, and Mary Boleyn, the elder sister of the famous Anne.

Catherine bore Henry many children, but only one survived. A daughter named Mary was born on February 18, 1516, who later became Queen Mary I in 1553. When Henry got tired of Catherine, he came up with every trick in the book to get rid of her. He eventually settled for the claim that their marriage was an unlawful union and sought to have it annulled. As we all know, the Pope refused to agree to this, so Henry took matters into his own hands. He made himself head of the Church of England and wanted to grant his own divorce, but Catherine put up her own defence. She argued convincingly that since her marriage to Arthur was unconsummated her union with Henry must be legal. By that time the King was in a more powerful position — sufficiently powerful to be able to get his divorce in 1533 and have Catherine banished from the court. She ended up a sad and lonely woman, dying alone on January 7, 1536. Because the proud and aggressive Catherine of Aragon stood up for her rights and didn't give in, a new word came into being that we still use today: arrogant. (Now, you may see other sources of this word, but it started in England with the divorced Catherine of Aragon.)

When King Richard II was old enough to be crowned with the gold hat, he had a portrait painted of himself sitting on the coronation chair in all his regalia. (If you happen to see the painting, notice that the chair hasn't got the lions placed under the feet. The Victorians added these.) This painting is the first known portrait of an English monarch. A likeness of a King was very rare this far back in history. (Richard was crowned on July 16, 1377.) Likenesses might be found on coins or even as a death mask, such as the one of Edward III. So with respect to this painting, it is fairly certain that it would be a true likeness. Richard donated this very painting to Westminster Abbey, possibly as a hint that he would like to establish a spot in there somewhere to be buried, and possibly with the knowledge that the painting would be safe. And well taken care of it certainly was. When you enter the minster, look to the right and there he is. He looks quite innocent, you might think. Well, let's put it this way: the first part of his reign, seven years or so, wasn't too bad. Then when his wife died without notice, he simply went downhill. Richard was yet another King who thought that all the power of running the country issued solely from the King's mouth, and none of it from Parliament. To cut a long story short, he returned from Ireland, was captured, taken to Pontefract Castle, and deposed. Henry Bolingbrooke took the gold hat and became known as King Henry IV.

What happened to Richard? He was either starved to death or, as Shakespeare claimed, murdered on February 14, 1400, then buried at Kings Langley, Hertfordshire. About thirteen years later someone said, "Pssst, did you know the chap had his portrait hanging up in Westminster Abbey?" So he was reburied in 1413.

Incidentally, Richard invented the handkerchief. Now my first thought is, what on earth did they use before that? Of course — that's why they had those big baggy sleeves.

Did you know that in the early days when the lords of the manor went a-hunting, upon returning they would immediately hand over the bagged game to their staff? The staff had to dress, skin, and cook the meat for the lords and all their guests, yet they themselves weren't allowed any of the meat from the game. All they got were the scraps and leftovers. The entrails, or internal parts, were called "umbles," and the cooks often made pies they shared with all the other staff. So it became a tradition that after a hunt the staff sat down to umble pie. This eventually became known as the poor eating "humble pie."

Did you know that in the early days in the pubs of England there was a box placed in a prominent position with a slot in the lid, and that on the front of the box was a sign that simply said: "To Improve Promptness"? It was customary for the clientele to drop a few coins in the box, which would benefit the waiters and, in turn, benefit the service, as the sign said. The sign was later abbreviated to T.I.P. This is where the word "tip" comes from.

During the 1600's, in the days of British rule in India, Queen Elizabeth I instituted the East India Company for trade. This trade was the impetus for the P&O (Peninsular and Oriental) shipping line that took the British to and fro. Now, how could one tell who were the wealthy passengers? Well, the first-class travellers would book passage on the ship so that their accommodations were portside outward bound and starboard homeward bound. This was to ensure that they always travelled in the shady part of the ship. So when the shipping clerks booked, apparently they would simply write the abbreviation rather than "portside outward starboard homeward." Thus, the word "posh" was created, which eventually came to mean "first-class people."

When in London on a Sunday you should visit a particular street market that's been in existence since the 1840's. It's in Middlesex Street, which was originally called Hogham Lane, situated between Aldgate and Bishopsgate. What's so special about this market? Well, it was established by some Jews who set up the silk weavers' trading area, and it became known as the place to buy seconds, or used items, in women's nightwear.

Today you can purchase clothes, fruit, toys, jewelry, and all sorts of goods. Even without buying anything, it's simply an experience just to wander down this famous street, which has adopted the name Petticoat Lane.

Here's another nursery rhyme that I'm sure most of you are familiar with. But have you any idea what it relates to?

"I had a little nut tree, nothing would it bear
But a silver nutmeg and a golden pear.
The King of Spain's daughter came to visit me
And all for the sake of my little nut tree."

Well, what this rhyme refers to is old Henry VII. His ambition was to make an alliance with Spain, and to achieve this he betrothed his eldest son Arthur, Prince of Wales, to marry the daughter of the King of Spain, Catherine of Aragon, who was just seventeen years old. Yet, as you know, Prince Arthur, who was next in line for the gold hat, died in 1502 without notice at the tender age of fourteen. Henry then thought about marrying his next son, Prince Henry, to her, but with only twelve years under his belt the lad was too young. When his own wife, Elizabeth of York, died, King Henry even thought about marrying the King of Spain's eldest daughter, Joanna of Castile, himself. But he'd heard that she had only "one oar in the water," as the saying goes. Catherine was hanging around, going through the motions of a princess, uncertain of what the future held. Then King Henry died on April 21, 1509. Prince Henry, now a handsome eighteen-year-old, wasted no time in marrying Catherine of Aragon, thus achieving his father's ambition by securing the alliance between England and Spain. Some say this was the wish the elder Henry had expressed to his son on his deathbed. So this story was the basis of the nursery rhyme.

By the way, did you know that in 1486, during the reign of Henry VII, playing cards were invented? He had a portrait of his wife, Elizabeth of York, printed on the cards as the Queen. This has appeared eight times on every deck of playing cards for over 500 years.

Now, we all know what happened to Catherine of Aragon. After being married to her for twenty-four years, Henry VIII divorced her on the grounds that the wedding was not legal. She was banished from the court and lived in Bedfordshire, where she ended up spinning lace. Some of her lady friends took up the craft, and this developed into a lace-spinning industry. Part of the equipment used during dark, stormy days was a three-foot candle, and during leisure breaks the younger men and women used such candles for a game they had devised. The idea was to light the candle and stand it in the ground. Then one by one they would jump over the lighted candle. The jumper considered it a success if he or she cleared the candle without putting it out. Apparently, a young lad named Jack was quite good at it. I expect you know which nursery rhyme relates to this game: "Jack be nimble, Jack be quick, Jack jump over the candlestick."

Did you know that Henry VIII wrote a book on the sacraments in reply to Luther? For this the Pope granted him the title "Defender of the Faith," a title that has been used by his successors. His full title was "By the Grace of God, King of England, France and Ireland; Defender of the Faith under God and of the Church of England and Ireland; the Supreme Head and Sovereign of the Most Noble Order of the Garter." Quite a mouthful, no?

Take a look at some British coins. You'll see the Latin words *Fidei Defensor, Fidei Def,* or *Fid Def* — or simply F.D. This shows that the present monarch still holds the position of Defender of the Faith.

Did you know that in the 1600's Cambridge University decided to admit commoners as students? Now, when students registered they were required to submit, in Latin, their social position. The commoners had to write the words *sine nobilitate,* which meant "without nobility." In time this term was abbreviated to "s. nob," which in turn became a term used to describe someone who was a pretender to a position. So this is where the word "snob" came from.

If you have an interest in ghosts, then you need to visit a wonderful building near Stratford-on-Avon. Take a short drive from Stratford down the Oxford road for about six miles, and without warning you'll come across a large turreted house, which is now called Ettington Park Hotel. It is described as a neo-Gothic mansion, and it was first mentioned in the famous Domesday Book in 1086. It has been in the Shirley family since way back in the early Norman period.

In 1983 it was converted into a luxury hotel at a cost of three and a half million pounds. In 1986 all the existing Shirley family members united at this great building to celebrate the 900 years it has been in the family. Obviously, an old building with so many centuries of character deserves to be haunted — and haunted it is. Several suspense movies have been filmed here: *The Haunting,*

The Turn of the Screw (with Wendy Hiller and Claire Bloom), *Watcher in the Woods* (with Bette Davis), and *The Omen*, to name just a few.

Now, let's talk about the present-day ghosts. One of the managers explains that when his duties included working in the bar, which was the old library, he was carrying a tray of drinks when suddenly a large book came out of the bookcase and landed on the floor in front of him, causing him to fall and spill the drinks. On several occasions this book has come out of the bookcase and has been simply placed on the floor, always opened to the same page. The book is called *St Ronan's Well*, Volume One, by Sir Walter Scott, and the page in question refers to a verse by William Wordsworth that goes "A merry place, 'tis said, in days of yore, but something ails it now — the place is cursed." So this literary ghost is perhaps trying to tell someone something.

Another apparition is that of one of the old maids who once worked there. She'd had a nasty fall down the stairs that took her life. One evening a guest at the hotel came to the bar in his dressing gown with wet hair and an extremely white face. He explained to the manager that while he was washing his hair, he looked in the mirror, and there sitting on the edge of his bathtub was a woman wearing a funny-looking cap and a grey smock with a ruff collar. This figure of the grey lady, as she is known, has been seen on many occasions. If you'd like the chance of seeing her, then stay at the Ettington Park Hotel and ask for the Stour Room. There have been many other sightings of this apparition at the hotel, but that room seems to be her favourite.

The manager also explains that one evening as he was

securing the building, he went into the snooker room and replaced all the cues and put all the balls into the various pockets. (No, not his pockets.) He switched off the lights and shut the door as he left. While he was in another part of the hotel, he heard the distinct sound of snooker balls clashing on the table. He went back to the room, turned on the light, and immediately spotted three balls on the table — with one still rolling along. He simply turned out the light and left the ghost or ghosts to their little game of billiards. (Now, that's what I call a good sport.)

Before I leave this famous place I'd like to mention one of the Shirley family members who, in fact, qualified for the Guinness Book of Records. He was a noted courtier who in 1677 was named Lord Ferrers of Chartley and, during the reign of Queen Anne, Viscount Tamworth and Earl Ferrers. Now there's a title for you. He had seventeen children from his first marriage and ten from his second. In addition to that, he also fathered thirty illegitimate children, for a total of fifty-seven offspring. Well, they didn't have TV in those days. Nor did he have a babysitter. He used a sheepdog instead.

Did you know that in the early days crying at one's wedding was expected? If the bride didn't cry then doom was cast on the couple's future. (Some people still believe that today.) The bride was watched carefully to make sure she genuinely cried. You see, people were convinced that a witch could shed only three tears and only from her left eye. So when the bride cried like a baby it was an assurance that she hadn't "plighted her troth." In other words, she had proved she wasn't a witch.

In the Middle Ages it was a custom to barter at the markets rather than mess around handing over money. Now, some of the farmers used to sell their piglets tied up in bags. But the more dishonest of them would replace the suckling pig with a cat. If the townsman was foolish enough not to inspect the bag at the time of the exchange, then it wasn't until he got home that he discovered his folly. And this is where the expression "letting the cat out of the bag" originated.

Did you know that Hampton Court was built by Cardinal Thomas Wolsey, the Lord Chancellor of England who also became Archbishop of York in 1514? Thomas Wolsey was the son of a butcher, and, according to history, was a hard worker. In fact, he graduated from Oxford University at the early age of fifteen. So for a young lad he certainly did quite well for himself. He started off as a chaplain to Henry VII, and then with Henry VIII he served as almoner before becoming a privy councillor. One could actually go on and on about his achieve-ments. But when you visit Hampton Court you'll notice in the Clock Court an outline of red bricks indicating where excavations revealed the foundations of an earlier construction. This was believed to have been the manor house of the Knights Hospitallers of St John of Jerusalem, from whom the Cardinal acquired the estate. So having torn that building down the Cardinal set out to build this magnificent palace. It has over 1,000 rooms and was once filled with great treasures, all of which were handed over to Henry VII. In my opinion, Henry went to dinner one night and, while waiting for the food to be presented, he started to wander around. When he realized that his Cardinal was living a far better lifestyle than he was, he made some very serious comments to Wolsey, who in turn wanted to stay in favour with Henry. So Wolsey said to the King, "Er, listen, Harry, as you like Hampton Court so much, let me make a present of it, and... er... you can have it." And Henry went running down the fields clicking his heels, shouting, "Yes!" At this point Hampton Court became a royal residence.

Hampton Court has several ghosts running around, three of them being the late wives of Henry VIII. His second wife, Anne Boleyn, who was beheaded on January 25, 1533, can be seen wandering around the corridors with her head under her arm. (You would have thought that by now she'd have found a cart to carry her head in.) Then there's "sweet Jane," as Henry referred to his third wife. She's the one who died after giving birth to Henry's only son on May 30, 1536. The other famous noisy ghost is Henry's fifth wife, Catherine Howard, who was beheaded on July 28, 1540, when she was arrested at Hampton Court. The guards had to physically drag her down the corridors to take her to the Tower of London. After a brief struggle she broke loose from the guards and went running and screaming after Henry, claiming her innocence and begging his forgiveness. Well, she's still doing that today.

Did you know that there's an easy way to remember what happened to each one of Henry VIII's wives?

"DIVORCED... BEHEADED... DIED... DIVORCED... BEHEADED... SURVIVED."

On a rainy Wednesday in 1690, the famous maze at Hampton Court was planted. This maze is so big that the average time to get to the middle is around twenty minutes. It usually seems to take longer to get out, which accounts for the huge holes in the hedges where people have clawed their way out in desperation. An average of 500,000 tourists visit Hampton Court each year, and the wear and tear is showing. There's talk of planting a new one.

Another old plant at Hampton Court, and one that seems to be doing well, is a 220-year-old grapevine. It has been protected in a greenhouse all these years. The grapes that are annually picked are sold to raise money for charity.

One old rhyming song was intended for the father who was always out drinking. It goes:

"Up and down the city road,
In and out The Eagle,
That's the way the money goes,
Pop goes the weasel."

The Eagle was an old-time music hall and tavern. The song tells of a father who is always going to the tavern to drink, wasting the family's money. The term "weasel" refers to someone who is neglecting his obligations. So in fact it's a person who isn't providing for his family.

Mary, Queen of Scots, was the daughter of James V and Mary of Guise. (Where on earth is Guise?) When she was sixteen, Mary was sent to France to be educated, and just ten years later she married the heir to the French throne, who became known as Francis II. Well, the marriage didn't last long. The French blueblood died two years later, in 1560, and Mary was sick as a parrot about it. The next year she moved back to Scotland. She had grown tired of eating snails and frog legs and yearned for porridge and haggis — and those confounded bagpipes. (No comments, please.)

In 1565 she married again, this time to her cousin, Lord Darnley. Most of her supporters rebelled when she did this. It wasn't long before she realised that Darnley lacked all the qualities of an intelligent and loving husband. And it was the last straw when he and some of his supporters burst into Hollyrood Palace and brutally murdered Mary's friend and secretary, David Rizzio, right before her eyes. You see, Darnley thought that Mary and David were having a bit on the side, and even though this wasn't the case, due to his jealous nature Darnley had decided to get rid of the secretary. (When in Edinburgh you can visit Hollyrood Palace and see the room in which this deed was committed.) Then in 1567 Lord Darnley himself was murdered. Mary married once again, now to the Earl of Bothwell. Well, many of the nobles believed that the Earl had been involved in the murder of Darnley, so Mary lost a great deal of support.

She was also cousin to Elizabeth I, and because of her plotting to take the gold hat from her cousin the Queen, she was locked up until it was decided what to do with her. During the nineteen years she was a prisoner, she was known to have done plenty of reading, praying, needlepoint, and gardening. Now, when she was gardening she was always accompanied by her four trusted handmaidens, who incidentally were all named Mary. (That surely must have been quite confusing when somebody called out "Mary.") There's a nursery rhyme that relates to her:

"Mary, Mary, quite contrary,
How does your garden grow?
With silver bells and cockle shells
And pretty maids all in a row."

By the way, an interesting fact is that her French husband, Francis II, apparently gave her a beautiful dress that was covered with embroidered cockle shells.

Here's another old rhyme:

"Oh, the grand old Duke of York
He had ten thousand men.
He marched them up to the top of the hill
And marched them down again."

Well, this one goes back to Frederick, Duke of York. He was the youngest brother of George IV, one of England's more awful Kings. The Duke was also one of the worst soldiers the country ever had. In the 1790's he was given an army of 30,000 men, whom he ordered to invade France to quell the revolution there. His idea was to save the French monarchy. Instead, he invaded Belgium and wasted over twenty months marching up and down the French borders, trying to work out how he was going to invade. Well, by the time the Duke came up with a plan of attack, the revolution was over. And to make things worse, the French revolutionary army attacked him and drove him back to England. Needless to say, Frederick got fired very diplomatically because he was a Duke. (If that had been you or I, they would have locked us up and buried the key.) But because of his royal dukedom, Parliament didn't want to upset him and make him look like an idiot. So they gave him a desk job, in charge of supplying troops with all their needs. Surprisingly enough, he made a good job of it and was liked by the troops so much that a statue was erected of him that still stands in Waterloo Place overlooking St James Park in London.

Now, having told you this story, here comes an interesting end to his end. When the grand old Duke of York died in 1827, he was given a state funeral. But the snag was that it was in the middle of winter, complete with thick ice and freezing weather. The funeral party left London in the afternoon in bitter cold to bury him at Windsor Castle in the chapel of St George. When the carriage with the coffin attempted to climb the big hill at Windsor, the horses pulling it skidded on the ice and, unnoticed by anyone, the coffin flew out the rear. When the funeral party arrived, everyone was relieved; they had been standing out in the cold long enough and just wanted to get the thing over with. You can imagine the shock when it was discovered that the Duke was missing. He hadn't shown up for his own funeral. So this meant more long delays while the troops went in search of the grand old Duke of York. The waiting dignitaries were diplomats, other lords and royals, military figures, and members of Parliament. And most were very old themselves. Just about all of them suffered afterwards from nasty colds, and several caught pneumonia. Out of the twenty-one people there, seven of them died not long after this incident. The grand old Duke of York is remembered for causing the deaths of more people when he was dead than he did when he was sent to war.

Talking about statues... did you know there is a large column called The Monument? This monument, erected in 1677, was designed by Sir Christopher Wren and is in memory of the Great Fire of London of 1666. Inside there's a spiral staircase 202 feet high. Its 311 steps are well worth climbing to get to a wonderful view of London. There was an inscription on the column stating that the fire had been started by a Roman Catholic Frenchman living in England who harbored an intense hatred of Protestants. Many people doubted his repeated declarations that he was responsible for the fire. Yet he was so persistent that the authorities finally said, "All right. All right." And then they hung him. Naturally, the Catholic Church was embarrassed by the incident and claimed that the man was insane and that the Catholics had nothing to do with the fire. Well, we shall never know.

Did you know that any law Parliament enacts has to first be approved by the Queen? Incidentally, the Prime Minister has an audience with the Queen every Tuesday, and nothing can become law until the Queen's seal is put on the document. This is done in the basement of the House of Lords in the Crown Office. It has always been the custom that no law is valid without the great seal; for this reason it is so closely guarded. Richard I's chancellor tried to recover the King's seal when it went down with a sinking boat, and he actually drowned trying to rescue it — such was its importance. Rebels stole Edward II's seal; with it they hoped to take the throne. Yet another seal was made to replace it. His son, Edward III, made counterfeiting the seal an act of treason. You can collect reproductions of some of the monarchs' great seals. Look out for them — they are great collectibles.

Did you know that the expression "the State Opening of Parliament" means the Queen is reenacting history? There's an old tradition that is carried out before the Queen can leave Buckingham Palace. A selected member of Parliament is escorted by car to the palace to be held "hostage" until the Queen is safely returned to Buckingham Palace. This act goes back to Charles II (1660–1685). He was the son of King Charles I, who at the age of twelve fled to France for safety. He was aware of what had happened to his father, who was deposed and executed, and he obviously was a bit on the cautious side. I can imagine him saying, "If I go to Parliament, I want to guarantee my return. So send me a top member of Parliament who will wait here until I get back." And that is exactly what happens even today: a member of Parliament has to hang around in the palace until the Queen returns — no doubt drinking a few cups of tea in grand style, poking around looking through the drawers, and generally being nosy.

While we're talking about Parliament, it's worth mentioning that the speaker of the House of Lords doesn't sit in a fancy chair but on a large red wool sack. This was introduced by Edward III as a symbol of England's great wool trade, which at one time was the country's principal export. Wool brought in an enormous amount of revenue for the country during the Tudor period. The Wool Acts of 1666 and of 1678 created new laws that upset a lot of people, especially the poor. The new laws stipulated that no corpses could be buried in an old shirt or any other garment that wasn't made of wool, and that the coffin was not to be lined with any other material but wool. Failing to comply would warrant a heavy fine or imprisonment. Elizabeth I introduced a law that people had to wear a woolen hat on the Sabbath day. This certainly helped the wealthy wool merchants get richer, and the taxes thus helped the country. So once again history repeats itself: the rich get richer and the poor get poorer.

Talking about old customs... another famous act is carried out each year on Maundy Thursday (the day before Good Friday). This is an old tradition that goes way back in history, based on the act of Jesus washing the feet of the poor. This tradition was and still is done by the Pope. But in England it was the custom of the reigning monarch to do it. In fact, it was done right up until James II (1633–1701).

Incidentally, the word "maund" means "basket," one of which was used by the Church to collect food for the poor during the feet-washing ceremony. Clothes, fish, bread, and even wine were given to the less fortunate during the reign of Elizabeth I. Then in 1688 the whole idea was dropped, not to be taken up again until 1936 by King George V.

The ceremony had always been held in Westminster Abbey, but now it is held in various cathedrals throughout the country. Also nowadays, instead of the poor being on the receiving end, special people are selected nationwide who have contributed an unusual amount of help to the various charities. And no, the monarch doesn't scrub your feet anymore — you have to clean your own. Neither is food and wine given away; instead, there are specially minted coins called "Maundy money," which are silver pennies, twopennies, threepennies, and fourpennies. (No, that hasn't been subjected to decimalization.) The Yeomen of the Guard are responsible for carrying the bags of coins, one white and one red, on silver trays held high above their heads, a custom based on when food was on the trays. (Well, you can imagine walking though a crowd of hungry poor people. By the time the guards got to the King the trays were empty. The poor thought it was a form of drive-through. This is why the trays were carried up high.)

Incidentally, one man and one woman for every year the Queen has lived is selected. So whatever her age is, double it and you'll have the total number of people who will receive this very old traditional coinage. And that's the Maundy tradition.

The Tudor period of English history is without a doubt my favourite period. England not only had a variety of colourful Kings and Queens during that time, but it was also relatively peaceful. During this era there were all sorts of cures and beliefs that seem very odd to us, but they were part of the lifestyle of our ancestors. Take, for example, the simple process of cleaning one's teeth. The people who did this used items such as crushed bones, powdered pumice stone, crushed coral or brick, or even soot. But they didn't use toothbrushes. Instead, they used a cloth or fruit peel to rub on whatever the concoction was, then they rinsed out their mouth with beer, sugary water, or wine.

Another practice was that of bloodletting. The doctors thought that letting the bad blood from one's body would relieve all sorts of symptoms, including pain. So when Queen Mary I became sick from depression her personal surgeon told her that he needed to relieve her of some of her blood. He simply cut into her arm then put a heated vessel over the cut to draw out the blood. Now, if she said she had a headache the doctor would prescribe drinking a mixture of lavender water, a bay leaf, some rue, roses, sage, and marjoram. "And if that doesn't do it, get hold of a used hangman's rope and wrap it around your head," he told her.

Now, a man who was bald might have preferred to stay that way after finding out what the so-called cure was: "Smear the grease of a goose and fox over your head, then wash it with crushed beetle juice, then finally rub it with garlic and vinegar." No wonder Mary, Queen of Scots, and Elizabeth I were both bald and had about eighty wigs each. A person who had hair and wanted to change its colour to blond was told that the best way to do it was to thoroughly rub in rhubarb and white wine and then sit in the sun. I bet the bugs and flies loved it.

Did you know that one of England's famous Kings was Edward III? He was a tall chap with long legs, and naturally his nickname was Longshanks. One thing about King Ed is that he was in love with his wife, who came from Spain. In fact, he went to Spain when he was only fifteen and visited King Alfonso X. Well, he must have made an impression because the Spanish King knighted him, then he wound up marrying the King's half-sister Eleanor, the Infanta of Castile. Now, the English found that their King had married a loverly lady, but they could not handle her name. Since it was such a tongue twister — Infanta de Castile — they came up with their own interpretation and nicknamed her "Elephant and Castle." So when you're in London and travelling on the "Tube," you'll see a place on the Underground map called Elephant and Castle. This is the suburb of South London named after King Edward III's wife. There's also a pub in the area bearing the same name.

Did you know that when George IV was a prince he was nothing but an overweight gambler and a very heavy drinker? In fact, the expression still used today of "drunk as a lord" is directly attributed to this pathetic King. He was a womaniser as well, constantly chatting up the ladies. And he also loved to eat — which certainly showed. Puddings were his favourite, and he ate them in quantities. For him the best one of all was suet pudding covered with sweet stuff. In fact, this is where we get the nursery rhyme:

"Georgie porgy pudding and pie
Kissed the girls and made them cry.
When the girls came out to play,
Georgie porgy ran away."

Now, what about this chap called King Arthur? Well, let's have a quick look at this legendary King from way back in history. The story all starts at Arthur's birthplace, Tintagel, Cornwall, 1,500 years ago. His birth was a result of magic. The story of King Arthur and his knights in shining armour sitting around a round table is a story of passion, love, noble and gallant deeds, chivalry, death and destruction, the sufferings of war, tragedy — the tale of a great King who loses not only his Queen, but also his kingdom and his life.

Yet have you ever stopped to consider why there exist such detailed accounts of Arthur, who supposedly was around during the fifth or sixth century? For the sake of contrast, consider William Shakespeare (1564–1616), the English dramatist and poet regarded as the greatest writer of all time, not just of England but of the entire world. The man is a household name, and he was born much more recently than King Arthur. Yet of this great literary figure we know very little.

Indeed, the whole legend of King Arthur is a wonderful story that has been dramatically told, written, and rewritten for well over a thousand years. (For instance, he was the one who made all that effort to pull the sword from the stone only to later throw it into a lake.) Writers have created this Celtic figure into a mould for future Kings. And many of the early Kings did attempt to live and rule in the chivalric style of this great man.

But how could he not have been great? With someone like Merlin at his side he should have ruled the world. (You'll notice that Merlin disappeared when Arthur married Guinevere. That deed made Merlin sick as a parrot, so he went back to the Welsh hills after telling Arthur to get on with it. I personally think he fancied Guinevere himself. But let's not start another story.) The tales of King Arthur are all based on information the storytellers and writers could get from early folklore. They've also been rewritten so many times by so many people and in so many languages that it makes one wonder what King Arthur will get up to next. Take, for example, that French poet, Chretien de Troyes. Seven hundred years after the so-called death of Arthur, this French chappie started rewriting the whole story — no doubt claiming that "It needs some romance and some knights in shining armour. And let's throw in a little royal scandal." And what about Sir Thomas Malory, the Yorkist knight who wrote the famous *Morte d'Arthur*, considered one of the great literary works of its time. Now, how's this for real scandal? Sir Thomas was locked up in prison when he wrote the tale because he'd been found guilty of theft, extortion, rape, and attempted murder. No wonder it was good — he had solid experience on which to base it all.

I don't want you to think I'm not a King Arthur fan. I've always loved to read about this legendary King. But I'm afraid that's what it is — a legend. Not many people I talk to like to hear that. Yet for centuries historians and archaeologists have been desperately and unsuccessfully trying to find reliable evidence that there was a King Arthur — let alone all that stuff he was supposed to have achieved.

Here's an interesting footnote. Did you know that King Henry VII named his eldest son Arthur? He died without notice, so next in line to the throne was the man known in history as King Henry VIII. Now, if Henry's brother had lived he would have been crowned King Arthur II. And who knows how he would have acted having the legends of King Arthur over his head?

And here's one last thought. Why did Arthur's kingdom disappear after his death? When a King dies, the kingdom usually lives on.

Another legendary character who was the subject of countless tales is Robin Hood. He was regarded in early Celtic history as the Green Man, a mysterious and sinister spirit that protected the thick forests covering most of England at the time. People avoided venturing into them because of the evil stories they'd heard all their lives. Dragons that fed on humans lurked in those forests. The Green Man who inhabited them was a hideous being that would destroy the life of anyone who dared to enter. Such tales were spread by the early Celtics and were generally believed. And when someone did enter the woods and not come out again... well, what other explanation could there be?

Of course, the truth of the matter was that such people got simply and hopelessly lost. Then some of those lost souls were probably attacked by wild beasts. Others, similar to what happens in our own time, were most likely mugged or even killed by strangers. The ones who did survive told incredible stories about their attacks, and some even blamed their misfortune on the so-called Green Man. Then the storytellers of the day would get hold of the tale and dramatise it, re-tell it, re-shape it, dress up in costume and play the part — and before long the entire story had been changed so much and told so artfully that people actually believed all they heard. Hence, a legend was born. (It's a bit like the press today, don't you think? When they get their teeth into a story, is it the whole truth or what they want us to read that's printed?)

Did you know that King George III spent several years wandering around the basement corridors at Windsor Castle? He acquired the habit of mumbling to himself, with occasional outbursts of laughter and shouting. He must have looked a sight with his long hair and his beard that nearly touched the floor. He always wore the same faded purple robe as he shuffled around, feeling his way around with a stick since he had gone blind as a bat. Not a very dignified way for a King of England to end up. He died on January 29, 1820.

What is a royal peculiar? (Please, no comments about Charles and Camilla.) No, I'm talking about Westminster Abbey, which is, by the way, not a cathedral, but an abbey and isn't run by the Church of England. It's different from the other great cathedrals around the country in that it's controlled by the head of the Church of England, Her Majesty the Queen, Elizabeth II. Now you may well be thinking: "What about the Archbishop of Canterbury? Doesn't he carry any weight?" Yes, he does, but not in Westminster Abbey. If he wants to go to the Abbey he must first seek permission from the Dean before setting foot inside it. This always holds true except for one event: the crowning of a royal monarch. As the leader of the Church, he's the only one with the authority to place the crown on a King or Queen, who is the head of the Church of England.

So how did all of this come about? Well, the origin of this unusual term, royal peculiar, is to be found in the time of Queen Elizabeth I. England was going through a period of religious friction that made Elizabeth's coronation a bit of a shambles. Henry VIII had dissolved the monasteries; the Benedictine monks had been kicked out and the secular priests had taken over some of the them (which were now called cathedrals). It was, in fact, on the same basis as St Paul's Cathedral, but money was used from Westminster to help support and make repairs to St Paul's. In 1556 Queen Mary I got in touch with Rome and, lo and behold, brought back Catholicism to England and the monks back to Westminster. When Mary popped her clogs (died, that is) on November 17, 1558, her half-sister Elizabeth I ascended to the throne. She kicked the monks out again, as she was all for the reformation of the Church in England. When she was crowned, on January 15, 1559, she was not amused. You see, the positions of Archbishops of Canterbury and York were vacant. So instead of having a high-ranking archbishop crown her, she felt disgraced having to settle for the Bishop of Carlisle to do the job. Why he was chosen, I have no idea. Maybe he was the only who could perform the service in Latin (for most of the service was spoken in this language). And she wasn't too happy with the anointing oil — she complained that it stank. When it came time for her to take communion the Queen disappeared for a while, no doubt sulking in one of the rooms or having a nice cup of tea with her feet up.

But to cut a long story short, in 1560 Elizabeth ordered that Westminster was no longer a monastery. So any monks still hanging around were thrown out, and the building was anointed with a new title: the Collegiate Church of St Peter in Westminster. And that's the official title even today. The Queen also decreed that the building should be run by a dean and have twelve prebendaries; that the school should have an upper master, one usher, and forty students; and that the church should have ministers, organists, and ten queristers, or choristers. (Today the school has about 600 pupils.) So because of this action taken by Queen Elizabeth I (the document of which, incidentally, she never did sign or seal), the running of Westminster Abbey is controlled by the Crown and doesn't get support from the Church of England. This is why a fee is charged to enter this magnificent building.

By the way, during the time the Collegiate Church of St Peter in Westminster was funding St Paul's Cathedral, a new saying emerged that we still use today: "robbing Peter to pay Paul."

Did you know that Florence Nightingale (1812–1910), known as "The Lady of the Lamp," was a great saviour for the troops in the hospital at Scutarri during the Crimean War? Her actions were an inspiration for an entire breed of women called Suffragettes. These were women who wanted to play an equal part in how things were being run. But not many people know that after arriving back from the war Florence Nightingale later ended up a hypochondriac. She claimed that her life was hanging by a thin thread — that she had a terrible heart condition and needed plenty of bed rest. And she stayed in bed for over fifty years. She eventually died, possibly of a heart attack, at the ripe old age of ninety. (Well, you can't be too careful.)

The nurses of St Thomas Hospital are called "nightingales." This hospital was first founded in the twelfth century as part of a priory, located opposite the Houses of Parliament. In this hospital you'll find the Florence Nightingale Museum.

Did you know that Big Ben — or, to use its correct title, the Clock Tower — is 314 feet tall and that the main bell, nicknamed Big Ben, is 9 feet in diameter and 7-1/2 feet high and weighs 13-1/2 tons? No wonder it silenced the original Londoners' clock found on Westminster Abbey. Each of the clock's faces is made of cast-iron and is 23 feet in diameter and has 312 pieces of pot opal glass. Each hour number is 2 feet long, the hour hand is 9 feet long, and the minute hand, made of copper, is 14 feet long. The minute hand travels a distance equal to 120 miles a year. There are 334 steps to the belfry and another 59 right up to the lantern, which is lit up each night that Parliament is in session.

The figures could go on and on. But instead, did you know that there's a prison in Big Ben intended for members of the House of Lords and the House of Commons who were noisy or rude during the debates? The last person to be imprisoned there was Charles Bradlaugh, a member of Parliament who refused to take the oath of allegiance to Queen Victoria in 1880. (From what I've heard and seen on TV, it looks like they should all be locked up for being too noisy.)

Did you know that Oliver Cromwell, who became Lord Protector of England after the execution of Charles I, was even offered the gold hat? "Would you please be our King?" asked the members of Parliament. But he replied, "No, after cutting the King's head off it wouldn't look good." And what a relief that was to the people of England. You see, Oliver wasn't a party animal — what with he and his followers being Puritans life was... well, to put it bluntly, miserable. When Oliver died on September 3, 1658, his son, Richard Cromwell, took over the position.

Yet the people had had enough. They wanted a real King. So after only six months Richard got the boot and Charles II, the son of the beheaded Charles I, took the crown. Now, the non-Cromwellians got together and decided to get their revenge on the man who had made their lives so wretched. They went to Westminster Abbey on January 30, 1661, and dug up Oliver Cromwell's body, dragged it through the streets, and ended up at Tyburn. They strung up the corpse by the neck for a good six hours, then laid it across a block and cut off the head. The body was then given to a large crowd that tore it to pieces, ripping off fingers, toes — anything that would act as a souvenir. For the finale they unceremoniously dragged what was left of the body down to the River Thames and tossed it into the water — just as most traitors end up. (And the fish in the Thames threw it back.)

Did you know that England, being an island, has been attacked from all sides by all sorts of people from all parts of the world? So it was inevitable that there would be a variety of languages. I'm sure the majority of the people didn't understand each other; thus, it must have been a relief when in 1362 what was then the English language replaced the French Norman. About twenty years later John Wycliffe and the Lollards (a religious group who opposed the Catholic Church) came up with the very first translation of the Bible into the English language. This was looked upon as being the birth of the English spoken in England today. (And about time, too.)

Scandal in the royal family is "old hat." When we wander through English history, we find that just about all the Kings and Queens were at it in one way or another. Consider the Viking King Edwy (Eadwig). He was crowned on November 23, 955, at Kingston-upon-Thames, which is southwest of London. (Remember that this is where the ancient Kings of England were once crowned, sitting on a large stone; hence, the name of the place means the town of the Kings on the River Thames.) One would have expected his coronation to be a sombre and religious affair. During the coronation feast the young King, who, incidentally, was only fifteen, was getting so bored with all the formalities of the speeches and the praying that he decided to slip off. He took advantage of everyone's heads being bowed in prayer to sneak out with a young lady whom he favoured and with her mother. The three were missing for a long time. The bishop and the nobles were getting a bit restless waiting for the young King to return in order to continue the ceremony, so they went looking for the lad. Lo and behold, they found him in his chamber completely naked, dipping his bread (going at it, that is) with the girl's mother while the daughter watched and demanded her turn. The crown was spotted on the floor unceremoniously lying on its side with a shoe sticking out of it. Well, the Bishop was sick as a parrot. It's rumoured that he boxed the lad's ears then dragged him off the women, who were oblivious of the bishop's presence. The King, after being instructed to dress and pop on the gold hat, was escorted back to the boring stuff. (Well, what would you rather be doing?)

While we're talking about young royals, how about this story that took place on January 15, 1478 — the date of a great royal wedding at St Stephen's Chapel in Westminster? Richard, Duke of York, married Anne Mowbray, who was heiress to the vast estates and fortune of her father, the Duke of Norfolk. Nothing wrong with that, you might think. What if I told you that the young chap was only four years old and his wife was only one year older? Well, permission apparently had been granted for this wedding by who else but the Pope. And if he said it was all right, one couldn't argue with that. (I wonder what they did on their honeymoon.)

When Henry VII defeated the notorious Richard III, he actually killed off the last of the medieval Kings of England. One thing Henry inherited was an empty treasury. So he put his meticulous mind for figures, as well as his treasurer, to work to come up with potential sources of revenue. And guess what they discovered. All the wealthy people had not paid any taxes for the last six years. And of course with such a tax break they had increased their wealth. (You see, nothing has changed: the rich get richer and the poor get poorer.) So Henry and his treasurer set off to see all these nobles, barons, and well-to-do merchants and to let themselves be entertained in a style befitting His Royal Highness. Great feasts accompanied by lavish entertainment were organised for this special guest, sometimes lasting two or three days. At each event the King's treasurer would tally up its total cost. Then when it was time to leave, Henry would give his generous host a whacking great big tax bill, which included fines imposed for excessive feasting. He made sure before he left that everyone properly acknowledged that he was their King and that their allegiance was to him only. He also made sure the host understood that he had to pay his taxes promptly or else suffer heavy fines. Then Henry and his treasurer would move on to the next wealthy person on the list. If a baron held back on his duty by providing less food than was appropriate, Henry would fine him heavily for having slighted the monarch. Thus, it was a no-win situation. The people knew where they stood in regard to paying their taxes, and by the time Henry VII died he was one of the wealthiest Kings that England had seen. And we all know who got his sticky little hands on the loot — our friend Henry VIII.

How about getting acquainted with the great castles of England? No matter where you're going, you'll no doubt pass by a castle while touring the country. To give you some idea of numbers, there are 511 castles in England alone you can visit. An additional 181 are in Scotland, and 82 are in Wales. So out of a total of 774 castles at least one is sure to interest you.

Now, how do you look at a castle? When you're wandering around one of these ancient buildings, try to imagine what it was like living in such a place during, say, the thirteenth century, without all the comforts of home you've left behind. Imagine that you partied with wenches and drank medieval margaritas, then woke up in the middle of the night needing to go to the bathroom. Would you feel your way along a wall looking for a light switch to see where you were going? And when you got there where would you do your business? What would you use for toilet tissue? And what about a nice hot shower or bath in the morning? How would you clean yourself? What about the food? With no refrigerators, how would you keep it from spoiling? All these questions should go through your mind as you're touring a castle. Or ask a guide these sorts of questions, if one is available. This will help you realise just how uncomfortable life was in those early days.

Each castle has a fascinating story. Some have more history than others. The Tower of London, for instance, is simply riddled with it. The best thing to do before visiting a castle is to study a little bit about it. Look up the monarchs, nobles, or knights who once lived there; who attacked the castle and when; and whether other royals or famous people visited the place. When you tour a castle armed with this kind of information, you'll be amazed how much more interesting your visit will be.

Visiting Stonehenge calls for a different viewing altogether. Since you can't get near what it is you want to see, it's difficult to get the feel of the place. In contrast, looking at a cathedral or a castle leaves nothing to the imagination as to what it is. Stonehenge... well, we just don't know what we're looking at. Although many books have been written about the place and people have done extensive research on this great monument, the stones "refuse to tell us what they are." (This is a phrase I use when giving tours at Stonehenge.) Going back to the seventeenth century, you find that Stonehenge was thought of as just a construction, though surrounded by many mysterious stories. A lot of people actually feared the place because of the superstitions linked to it — including the notion that it had great healing powers. During the early seventeenth century a hardware store in Salisbury produced a handout and poster advertising for interested people to "come and purchase a hammer and chisel to take to Stonehenge to chip a piece of healing rock." Included was a long list of what the rock would cure: "Tiredness, Forgetfulness, Deafness, The Weakness of Any Member, Pockes, Hectic Flushes, Apoplexies, Lethargies, The Scratch," as well as many other maladies. And if you took a larger piece of the rock and threw it down your "well," it would rid you of all vermin and give you clear water. (Yeah, right. I wonder if it would do anything for mothers-in-law.) Keep this tidbit of history in mind when you look at those great monolithic stones and see places where people have used a chisel. Keep in mind as well the fact that there were probably large chunks lying around that have also been taken for whatever reason.

But getting back to the origin of Stonehenge, just consider the size of the stones. Some of the larger ones in the centre stand over twenty-two feet high and weigh forty-five to sixty tons each. And imagine how much they weighed before they were shaped. Without modern machinery, how were they possibly moved? You must ask yourself this as well as other questions about Stonehenge. But be careful about the answers. Many people will tell you what they think of this great question mark in English history, and this is good. New interpretations and ideas are being circulated all the time. Yet what I'm leading up to is that no one has the right to tell or dictate to you what Stonehenge signifies because nobody knows. Stonehenge can be whatever you want it to be.

Having said that, I suggest you listen to some of the stories told by the guides, or, if you're part of an escorted tour, ask the tour director for his or her view. Some of the guides will make sense and others... well, you know what I mean. Yet it will give you an idea of what has been said about this structure.

Stonehenge isn't the only circle of stones in Great Britain. There are over 900 of them in all shapes and sizes scattered around the country. Of these, the most famous is, of course, Avebury. It's a much bigger circle of stones, complete with a village within it. Yet at this site, unlike Stonehenge, you can at least walk around and touch most of the stones. It's difficult to imagine, but the original ditch around Avebury was thirty feet deep, and its banks were as high as twenty feet. In the early days it must have been very impressive; but many of the stones were destroyed over the centuries. The smaller ones were pushed over and buried. "Who was responsible for this?" you might ask. Well, it was the Church. When the village was formed, the Church authorities simply did not like the competition caused by this pre-Christian worshipping ground; so they organised a destroying party. They surrounded the big stones with brush and lit a fire, waited until the stones were red-hot, then threw water over them, which caused them to crack or split wide-open. Some fell over on their own. One large stone was found to have a doctor's remains underneath it. He might well have been there just in case there was an accident — or was it a bit of pagan revenge? So if you sit and look at it today, with a nice cup of tea, try to imagine what this place must have looked like and, of even more importance, how it was used. The Alexander Keiller Museum at Avebury contains many interesting artifacts that will help you with whatever ideas you come up with. Just about all of the circles, riddled as they are with legends and myths, have an interesting story to tell. (But of course they're stories you must take with a pinch of salt.) You'll also find that some of these great circles have healing powers and that if you were to walk into the centre of them with a metal divining rod the energy forces would throw you out. Well, you try it then!

Here's one final thought for readers who have visited Stonehenge or else have studied the subject. The great Heele stone supposedly carries great significance. As the sun rises on June 22, which is the Summer Solstice or Midsummer Day, it appears to sit on top of this Heele stone when viewed through the large upright stones that are shaped exactly square and capped with a "hinge" stone. (By the way, this is where the name Stone-hinge comes from, although it was corrupted and eventually became "Stonehenge.") Yet if this stone is truly the most important feature of the event, then why wasn't it shaped to precision as the other stones were? I'd be delighted to hear your view on the subject.

A Light-Hearted Look at the History of England

WHAT HAPPENED DURING THESE IMPORTANT ERAS OF ENGLISH HISTORY:

1,400,000 BC A hairy little man rubbed two sticks together and discovered fire.

500,000 BC Another little hairy man saw an animal walk past him, without saying "hello," so he killed it and discovered food.

25,000 BC An even hairier man dropped his kill in the fire and discovered cooked food.

20,000 BC Then along came a smart alec who got fed up with dragging his food and his woman home, so he invented the wheel, then sat around for a few more years waiting for someone to invent another one.

10,000 BC Instead of throwing rocks to kill food, spears and other weapons were invented — for this purpose, and for self-defense.

8,600 BC Another smart alec saw a seed fall to the ground and sat around to watch it grow, (Well, there was nothing else to do) and lo' and behold, planting stuff was invented.

8,400 BC With all the wild animals running around, man realized that he could train them to his advantage, and so man's best friend came into history: the hunting dog.

5,000 BC England broke away from the rest of Europe. (Well it was those French... what with eating all those frogs legs... and what about those snails? No... we were better away from all that, thank you!)

2,500 BC The Vikings had discovered how to make use of all their weapons and were just waiting for someone to invent boats so they could go do stuff.

1,500 BC This was the period that the Bronze Men (no, it doesn't mean they were people with good tans) came over to England and started carving graffiti horses and stuff along the banks of hills, no doubt establishing their spot.

1,400 BC Primitive man started painting those pictures in the caves, knowing, one day, modern man would find them and stand there, amazed. Wonder where we get our ideas for graffiti from today?

1,000 BC Here was another case of a smart alec who, having skinned an animal, wore the skin to keep himself warm. He thought, "What a good idea I have thought of." Then someone threw a spear at him thinking he was an animal. You'd think he would have taken the head off before wearing it, wouldn't you?

500 BC Man started building structures to live in, instead of those stinky, smoke-filled caves. So, here we had the introduction of carpenters.

100 BC Primitive man started living in their new style dwellings with ONE woman — you see, three or four women was getting a bit too much to handle, so they settled for just the one — and here was the introduction to Mothers-in-Law.

55 BC Things were going along just nicely when, all of a sudden, along came these strange looking chaps with shiny helmets, leather skirts, funny sandals and a use for two wheels: a chariot. Also, fancy swords, new women, wine, and solid buildings to live in. Thousands of these chaps running all over the place! This, of course, was the introduction of the Romans.

43 AD Now, after the Romans had a look around England, they took a fancy to the country, so they took it. This was the introduction of "stealing." They took over most of the country and developed the large cities that we know today, Examples: Londinium (London); Eboracum (York); Aquae Sulis (Bath); Lindum (Lincoln) and many others.

60 AD The people of England suddenly realized that these chaps, dressed in leather skirts and shinny hats were not British, so, led by an attractive women and her two daughters, they decided to throw them out. This woman was known as Queen Boudica. She got really annoyed when she asked the Romans to leave and they refused. So, she killed 75,000 Roman troops and then burnt Londinium to the ground. This was the discovery of P.M.S.

122 AD The Romans did not take the hint and decided to stay. You see, these chaps were sharp people, hence the term "Roman Nose." Anyway, some smart alecs decided to wander up to the north of the country and they came across Scotland. Well, Emperor Hadrian saw a bunch of chaps running around in cloth skirts, with blue faces, blowing bagpipes and eating haggis. (Well, they say first impressions...) Without hesitation and all in one breath, he said: " Build a wall to keep these chaps away from mine." Hence, we have Hadrian's Wall. (I wonder if he had a permit to build that thing?)

143 AD A mate of Hadrian came along and built another wall much further up into Scotland, just to make sure these chaps were kept up in the mountains where they belonged. This wall is called Antonine Wall.

209 AD England got its first Martyr, Saint Alban, who was beheaded on the spot where the Cathedral stands. He was a priest, trying to convert the people of Alban to Christianity, so the Romans converted him. The city bears his name: St Albans.

313 AD Then along came this Emperor Constantine and gave the thumbs up to Christianity and acutely encouraged religion. The only people he could not stand were the Druids. Anyone who walks around wrapped in a tablecloth and wearing a pointed hat, well... To the Romans this was very suspicious.

407 AD The Romans eventually got fed up with England. They built about a thousand big ships and laden them with everything and anything they could get there sticky little fingers on and off they jolly well went, leaving England with all those fine buildings and 5,000 miles of roads, two great big walls in Scotland and thousands of little tea shops in Devon and Cornwall. Legend has it that they left one great man to look after the place and keep up the payments on the buildings. He pops up later in history.

410 AD Now this period in history is known as the "Dark Ages." It should have been the dark ages when those Italian chaps were there. (You know what I mean — dark skinned.) The term Dark Ages means that there was not much recording going on as regards getting history written, since journalists had not yet been thought of.

500 AD Word got around that the Romans had left and this news opened the flood gates for all sorts of immigrants who didn't have to worry about customs, passports, and green cards. They just came on over from all over the place. Some were called Celts, Jutes, Saxons... and remember, these chaps brought with them all their cultures, vices, diseases and religions *and* those revolting turkey legs! (Oh, sorry. That was much later.)

500 & Bit This is when England saw this Romano-British King called Arthur. He was the chap I mentioned earlier, left by the Romans (who must be aging well). He, apparently, did not like these Saxons trying to bully their way around the country, so he fought a battle just about everywhere in England. He certainly left his mark.

555 St. David converted the Celtic Welsh people to Christianity and that started them off singing and they have been doing it ever since. Some people tried to dig caves, to hide from all that singing going on and discovered a black rock formation. Thus, Coal was found. (Mind you they didn't know what to do with it, but at least it was discovered.)

565 Another saint was running around Scotland. Long before he was a Saint, Mr. Augustine, (who invented August), was sent to England by Pope Gregory and told to sort out and convert the Scottish people. I think when the Romans went back, some smart alecs went gossiping to the Pope, telling tales on how they spoke, dressed, and well, I think it was that Haggis that did it. Soon as the Pope heard about all this, he was sick as a parrot and shouted to August: "On your bike — go and deal with them!" And he did — converted them to brewing whiskey instead of Haggis.

830 Now, the Vikings got the hang of this King stuff and before long there were Kings all over the place. The policy was that he who wields the sword mightier than another can be King. England had seven Kings that we know of and may well have had other Kings lurking around that were not recognized by early historians. So, this was the start of costly Monarchs — not one, but *seven* of them.

891 One of our very early Kings was a great chap because he got serious about recording history and was responsible for writing the Saxon Chronicles. You see, he wanted people much later on to read that he was a "Great King." That became his title: "King Alfred the Great," but apparently he was a lousy cook. The great King was lying on his death-bed drinking a bottle of medieval Guinness when his children asked the great one, "Where would you like us to bury you, when you pass on?" The great King Alfred with half-closed eyes, raised his bottle up high and in a weak voice cried out. "I will finish this bottle of Guinness and throw it to the wind — wherever it lands, bury me." So, they buried him on top of the closet.

940 This was a period in history when England had a whole bunch of boy Kings. To explain... as I mentioned before, many Kings during this period where quite ruthless and having so many Kings running around was simply asKing for trouble. Each King would try to out-smart the other and take all of his kingdom. Then, to make sure that the ruthlessness would continue, the eldest son would succeed. These are the five boy Kings in question: 940-946 — Edmund the Elder; 946-955 — Edred; 955-959 — Edwy The Fair; 959-975 — Edgar The Peaceful; 975-978 — Edward The Martyr. (This is where the saying, "What's in a name?" came from.)

991 This was when a smart alec King called "Ethelred The Unready" came along. He came up with the very first tax, because he was he didn't want to do battle with anyone who invaded the country — he simply paid them off. This was the introduction of the people being robbed by their leaders. (Take note, history repeats itself.) The King couldn't pay them all off and got very tied of these Danes coming over to pillage and rape and get paid for it. So, he had all the Danes in the country killed. Well, you might have guessed: The Danes waged a full-

scale war. And what do you think Ethelred The Unready did? He rushed off to catch a ferry to Normandy, which he nearly missed because he was still Unready.

1013 The Danes staged a full- scale invasion of England and took the throne."Who is the King?" you might ask... His name was Forkbeard The Dane, (sounds like a pirate) then along came another King after him called King Canute. This chap was looked upon as being a very powerful man, "Why, he can even stop the sea from coming in if he commanded it." Not being the sharpest knife in the drawer, the King sat on his throne at the sea shore and commanded the tide to stop coming in. (This is where we get the term, cold feet.)

1042 The Pious King Edward The Confessor was the next great King of England he established the Palace of Westminster and the Abbey. He also announced that his cousin William would be his heir when he pops his clogs. Well when he was on his death bed another cousin of the King's pops in, with a bunch of grapes, to see him and asked the King to appoint him as the next King of England. Rather than that Norm chap, and the King agrees. (You see what a bunch of grapes will do.)

1066 This is a date that echoes down in English history — a date when most historians start talking about the Kings and Queens of England. This date, for me, is the most important battle of all battles that have been fought. It was the turning point in the English history, and — lets face it — history is wrapped around the Kings and Queens of England. Remember this statement from William Shakespeare's Richard II? Act 3, scene 2: Richard speaking:

"Let us sit upon the ground and tell sad stories of the deaths of Kings: how some have been deposed, some slain in war, some haunted by the ghosts they have deposed, some poisoned by their wives, some sleeping, killed. For within the hollow crown that rounds the mortal temples of a King, keeps death his court and there the antic sits, scoffing at his state and grinning at his pomp, allowing him a breath, a little scene to monarchies, be feared and kill with looks, infusing him with self and vain conceit, as if this flesh which walls about our life were brass — impregnable, and humored thus, comes at the last and with a little pin, bores through his castle wall... and... farewell King!"

So, those few, simple, great words just about sum it all up. To understand England, you must first understand the Kings and Queens. (Well, having said that, I don't think we will ever understand Prince Charles.)

Useful Historical Information About Great Britain

PREHISTORY PERIOD	**c 250,000 BC to 43 AD**
BRONZE AGE	**c 1700 BC to c 650 BC**
IRON AGE	**c 650 BC to 43 AD**

ROMAN PERIOD

BC 57 – 54 During this era the Romans made several attempts to raid the country, but for some reason they gave up and went home. Maybe it was too cold for them running around in those skirts they wore.

AD 43 The Romans landed in England and started a full conquest of the country, taking all the major towns.

c 60 Queen Boudicea and her two daughters revolted against the Romans, killing 75,000. She then burnt Londinium (London) to the ground.

c 122	Emperor Hadrian built a great wall separating Scotland from England. The other wall that people confuse it with is called the Antonine Wall, which began around 143.
c 313	Another Emperor, Constantine, was known as "The Great." This was the chap who recognized Christianity.
c 409	The Romans got sick of England, so they packed up all their things, stole whatever they could get their sticky little fingers on, then went back to Italy, where the weather was a little warmer, no doubt.

THE DARK AGES

c 410 – c 650	Called the "Dark Ages" because very little of what-was-what was recorded. So we have no proof of history. Remember, this was a period of legendary stories and, of course, the Celts. The Celts and the famous Druids were, in fact, the people of England.

SAXONS & VIKINGS

c 410	From the period of c 410, as soon as the Romans had left England and slammed the door behind them, lo and behold, a whole bunch of other

invaders were hanging around ready to invade. They were a crowd called the Angles and Jutes from (where else?) Germany and Denmark.

c 500 – 600	This was known as the "Heroic Age," when we had this great King Arthur chap. It has been claimed that he was left by the Romans to keep the peace.
c 600's	All the new invaders claimed their bit of the country, so primitive England had to suffer not one royal family but seven of them. This was called "The Saxon Heptarchy."
c 829	Then there was King Egbert, who thought he was greater than the others. He called himself King Egbert, King of Wessex, and Overlord of all England.
c 870 – 880's	During this period we had yet another famous King, Alfred the Great, who won great victories in the eastern part of the country by defeating the pesky Vikings. He also established the Danelaw.
c 937	King Athelstan won a great victory over the Vikings and the Scots at Brunanburh.

c 940 – 978 During this period the country saw five boy Kings. They were King Edmund, King Edred, King Edwy, King Edgar and King Edward.

c 1013 We had a King called Ethelred, known as "The Unready" and "Ill-Advised." He had big problems with the Danes, who deposed him as King. (The name Ethel-Red has two meanings: Ethel means Noble, and Red means red hair and ruddy complexion.)

Also in 1013, another rare King called Forkbeard — who was a Dane — led a full-scale invasion of the country to secure his position.

c 1016 During this era we had the famous King Canute, who was King of all England and the Scandinavian Empire. He was the King who tried to tell the tide to stop, but got his feet wet and was embarrassed. This was, if you like, the first "Royal Flush."

c 1050 Then there was the great King Edward, "The Confessor." He told William, Duke of Normandy, that when he "popped his clogs" he, William, could have the Kingdom of England, thus making William his heir.

c 1066 The Battle of Hastings made this one of the most famous years in English history. King Harold, who took the crown when Edward the Confessor died, caused this battle. Remember, William was promised the kingdom. During this year William, Duke of Normandy, defeated Harold, claimed the crown, and became King William I of England.

NORMANS

1066 – 1154 The Battle of Hastings was over and King William I started ruling England with an iron fist. He was known as "The Conqueror." He lived up to his name and ordered the compiling of the Domesday Book. He also left us the Tower of London.

1087 This was the year that William II took over as King — and what a pathetic chap he was! He should have been sent on the Crusades to keep him away from England. He was killed while out hunting and it was recorded as an accident. (Yeah... right.)

1100 During this year William's brother Henry took over wearing the gold hat. (By the way, Henry was with the hunting party when his brother was shot in the heart with an arrow... You don't think that... No, you see there is no evidence. Here is a pattern that appears throughout history with the royals.) Henry I's only son, heir to the throne, was drowned in the King's "white ship."

1135 Henry I died and the throne went to his nephew, Stephen. This was the reign about which the historians wrote: "God and his angels slept for nine years." Henry I was another tragic King.

MEDIEVAL PERIOD

1154 Another Henry, the Second, came to the throne after Matilda's reign, which lasted only seven months. A lot of historians didn't record her reign. Henry II is known in English history for making Thomas Becket famous. (Now there's a name that rings loudly in English history!)

1189 Richard I got his sticky little fingers on the crown. Then, after making the country bankrupt, he set off on the Crusades, just to glorify his name. He was King of England for ten years and guess how much time he spent in the country? Only ten months! Yet everyone sings his praises. These people ought to read the whole truth about him.

1199 This is the time of the great King John's reign. Despite all the early nonsense that was written about him, it's now been proven that John was not as bad as the historians had branded him. He was forced to seal the Magna Carta, but if you really study this document you will see that most of it was for the baron's benefit.

1209 King John was excommunicated which meant that he could not talk to God. How they do that, I have no idea.

1216 Henry III is remembered for helping to create the English Parliament. He was also responsible for building much of the tower of London. (Not the white tower, but most of the present structure.) Henry III was, in a nutshell: ambitious, cultured, and arrogant. He was also reported to be a coward — but apart from that he was a good lad.

1272 The first great King Edward I conquered Wales and offered himself as their leader, but they refused, saying they wanted "someone who was born in Wales and speaks the Welsh tongue." Without hesitation, Edward went into Caernarfon Castle where he held his newborn son in his upturned shield and cried out to the Welsh people, "I give you my son, who was born in Wales and does not speak English." the Welsh agreed.

He also tried to conquer Scotland and thus came to be known as "The Hammer of the Scots." So says the epitaph on his tomb in Westminster Abbey

1307 Edward II was the complete opposite of his father. One of the worst Kings to sit on the English throne, he allowed Robert the Bruce to defeat the English at the battle of Bannockburn. He was gay and spent most of his time with his fancy men instead of looking after his affairs of state. He was eventually deposed and murdered in Berkeley Castle.

1327 King Edward III was, like Edward I, a great warrior King. At age fourteen he took the crown. It didn't take many years for him to avenge his father's death by sneaking into Nottingham Castle through secret passages accompanied by four of his trusted knights. He found his mother with Roger Mortimer and killed him then sent his mother to Castle Rising in Norfolk for the rest of her life. Also, during Edward's reign, the "Hundred Years War" began against — who else? — the French.

1377 Richard II was another boy King, ascending to the throne at ten years of age. As with the others, he was dominated by his advisers and the nobles of the country. Richard II levied heavy taxes. Later on in life he was forced to abdicate. Then he was tucked away in a small room in the Tower of London where he was eventually... yes...

murdered. His official portrait is the one hanging on the wall to the right as you enter Westminster Abbey.

1399 Henry IV... You may have heard of The War of the Roses. It was a question of which rose do you like, red or white? The Yorks fancied the white rose while the Lancasters rather liked the red. Inevitably, war broke out between the two sides. Henry's wife, Margaret, played a big part in this war since Henry... well... he "only had one oar in the water," if you know what I mean. He suffered badly from epileptic fits and eventually died of leprosy, syphilis, and eczema, all combined with gout.

1413 Henry V was quite a popular King who transformed the country into the strongest nation in the whole of Europe. He sorted out the rebelling Welsh and won a great victory at the Battle of Agincourt, retaking Normandy and thus becoming next in line for the throne of France. Henry was a brave and loyal leader but, on the other hand, he was harsh and ruthless in commanding what was to be done.

1422 Henry VI was another boy King, who ascended to the throne at only nine months old. A special gold hat was made for him for his coronation. The country was ruled for him and when he got older they found that he wasn't the sharpest knife in the drawer — there was a bit of insanity creeping in. Eventually, he was deposed and was given a nice little room in the "medieval motel," also known as the Tower of London. No prizes for guessing what happened next... yes... he was murdered. But at least the War of the Roses was over.

1461 Edward IV became the first monarch of the House of York. He beat the pants off the Lancastrians at the Battle of Towtown. (No, not Toytown.) The Lancastrian Henry, who was hoping to take the crown, found himself locked up in a little room (where they left the light on for him) and guess what happened to him? They murdered him. Edward had ten children by his wife Elizabeth Woodville.

1483 Edward V, within a very short time after becoming King (he was only twelve years old), fell victim to his wicked uncle, Richard Duke of Gloucester, who was desperate for power. So, once again, guess what medieval motel he put the young King in? Yes, the Tower of London — along with his brother, who was only nine years of age. And guess what happened to them both? Yes, murdered. All because Richard wanted to wear the gold hat and have the power of a King.

1483 Richard III got his wish. He became King of England and was the last of the medieval monarchs. Before he became King, he had anyone who was a threat to the throne and everyone who questioned his imprisonment of young Edward put to death in the Tower by having their heads chopped off — even if they were related to him or to Edward. But revenge is sweet. Richard III was killed at the Battle of Bosworth in 1485. There his body was stripped and badly beaten, then put in the back of a horse-drawn cart and dragged off to the city of Leicester, where he was buried in an unmarked grave.

TUDOR

1485 Henry VII was the chap who won the crown from Richard III and became the first monarch of the Tudor period. Henry stabilized the country, which had been dragged into debt by Richard III, and restored the government. He was very thrifty with money and kept an eye on all the income — checking the books himself.

His eldest son, Arthur, was heir to the throne but died suddenly "without notice." This paved the way for the next eldest son, Henry, who was heading for the Church. During Henry VII's reign he managed to make treaties with both France and Scotland. He died, having suffered from arthritis and gout.

1509 The famous Henry VIII was not the best King we ever had, but he was the best known — mainly for his invention of "wife disposal." He was a very forceful King who didn't get what he wanted from the Pope, so he broke with Rome and became head of the Church of England himself. He is also credited with building a fine navy, which ended up with over fifty-three warships. Henry VIII is also famous for his closing of 823 monasteries, which put a lot of monks out of business. His leg had ulcers that made him very irritable and dangerous.

1547 Edward VI, the only son of Henry VIII, was a sickly child. He did authorize the first "Church of England Prayer Book," and had he lived, would have no doubt made a fine King. He was only nine years old, and was dominated by his uncles and nobles, who virtually ran the country until his death. Edward was asked by his uncle, the Duke of Northumberland, if he would consent to grant the throne to the Duke's daughter-in-law, Lady

Jane Grey. This was meant to stop Edward's half-sisters, Mary or Elizabeth, from taking the crown. Edward agreed. Then he died. I believe that Edward's medication had something slipped into it to get rid of him so he couldn't change his mind. He died of tuberculosis on July 6, 1553.

1553 Lady Jane Grey was sixteen years old, very intelligent and beautiful. She was another victim of a plot to usurp the throne. She was forced to marry Lord Guilford Dudley. After only nine days as Queen, the Lord Mayor of London proclaimed that Mary should be Queen. Because Jane had few supporters, she had to step down. And guess where she was sent? Yes... another visitor to the Tower. She was beheaded, along with her husband, for treason.

1553 Mary I was nicknamed "Bloody Mary." Her main goal was to convert England to the Catholic religion. She ruthlessly tried to suppress Protestantism in the country and burnt over 283 Protestant martyrs. She lost Calais, our last foothold in France. (Mind you, if you have ever been to Calais, well...we didn't lose much.)

Mary married Prince Philip of Spain — that didn't go down well with the people of England. She had no children, though she desperately wanted them. She died of influenza after reluctantly agreeing to hand the throne over to her Protestant half-sister, Elizabeth.

1558 Elizabeth I, the Virgin Queen: "Gloriana" and "Good Queen Bess" were the names she was lovingly called. Her greatest victories were the defeat of the Spanish Armada and re-establishing the Protestant religion. She survived many plots devised by the Catholics, even lead by her cousin Mary Queen of Scots, whom Elizabeth eventually had executed. She reigned for over forty-four years.

Elizabeth kept putting sulfur powder over her face, which was slowly eating her skin away. She thought it made her look white and pure, but close up it must have been a sight. She had no hair on the back of her head and her teeth were as black as the ace of spades. She eventually died of blood poisoning in March of 1603.

STUART

1603 James I (also James VI of Scotland) suffered threats from Catholics when they tried to blow up Parliament on November 5, 1605. He authorized the translation of the Bible that is still known as the "King James Bible." He hated the Puritans and finally told them to get lost... which they did. They established one of the first permanent English colonies in North America, named after James I, called Jamestown.

King James preferred the company of men and believed he — not Parliament — had the divine right of God. He died of kidney failure and left the crown to his son, Charles.

1625 Charles I, was five feet, four inches tall, prudish, shy, shifty and had a habit of stammering when excited or in a temper. He, like his father, thought that he was under the direct rule of God, not Parliament. In fact, he dissolved Parliament on three occasions and from 1629 to 1640 ruled without them.

Civil War broke out, and the first battle was fought at the Battle of Edge Hill, October 23, 1642. Both sides claimed victory, but eventually the King was defeated and captured. He became the first King of England to lose his head.

1649 Oliver Cromwell ruled during this period in English history, known as "The Commonwealth," under the title of Lord Protector. After a while the people of England got a bit tired of the very strict rules of a Puritan. After Cromwell died on September 3, 1658, a search party was sent to France to get hold of Charles I's son, who was next in line for the crown. England was desperate to get its monarchy back, and did.

1660 Charles II was known as the "merry monarch." This period in England is known as the Restoration. The English rejoiced at Charles I's coronation and found that their new King was knowledgeable and witty. But, sadly, he was pleasure-seeking and disloyal to his wife, Catherine of Braganza, and to his ministers. During his reign came the Great Plague in 1665. Then, to crown it all, there was the Great Fire of London in 1666. Charles II died of uremia and mercury poisoning.

1685 James II... during this period in English history the country saw a dramatic change in religion. The King decided to change his religion to Catholicism and gave all the good positions to Catholics only. This sparked the Glorious Revolution which encouraged the Protestant, William of Orange, to come over with an army. Many of James' army had fled to France and eventually the King did the same. Parliament declared that James had abdicated, putting the crown up for grabs. Meanwhile, James turned up via Ireland with a French army and hopes of getting his gold hat back, but he was heavily defeated by William at the Battle of the Boyne. James went back to France with his tail between his legs, sick as a parrot, and died of a stroke.

1689 William and Mary... if you're wondering where William fits in the royal line, well, he was the nephew of James II. The people of England seemed to be quite happy with William, who was a great hero in Holland for driving out the pesky French who kept invading. (What on earth got into those French people? They were always trying to annoy somebody, somewhere.)

Now "Who is this Mary?" is your next question. Well, she was the daughter of James II, and this was one of the few occasions that England had a King and a Queen. In fact, Mary was running the country while William was abroad. She administered the government very well using the King's advice until she died at Kensington Palace, December 28, 1694. As for William... well, he was not very popular with the Scottish Highlanders because he allowed the massacre at Glencoe. They celebrated when they heard that William's horse had stumbled on a mole hill, which resulted in his death on March 8, 1702 at Kensington Palace.

1702 Anne was Mary's sister. One of the saddest things about Anne's reign is that she desperately wanted children, but none of them lived. They either died in childbirth or not long after. She actually gave birth to seventeen children and only had one who survived until his ninth birthday; then he died when he got too excited at his own birthday party. Anne was also the Queen that gave that tremendous palace to the Duke of Marlborough for his victory at the Battle of Blenheim. You can see the Blenheim Palace today when visiting Woodstock at Oxfordshire. Queen Anne died at Kensington Palace of a stroke. This was the end of the Stuart Line.

GEORGIAN PERIOD

1714 George I... In the history of the Kings and Queens of England we had been ruled by the Danish, the Normans, the French, the Welsh, the Scottish, and a Dutchman. What did England do to deserve this old, fat lump from Germany, who couldn't speak a word of English? He spent most of his reign in Hanover and was a sad excuse for a royal. His mother was Princess Sofia, who was the grand-daughter of James I. During George I's reign, England experienced the first Industrial Revolution and the first proper Prime Minister, Sir Robert Walpole. George also imprisoned his wife for life because he suspected her of having an affair. In my book he was a total disaster for England.

1727 George II was yet another King born in Germany, but at least he spoke a little English. He also relied on his Prime Minister, Sir Robert Walpole, and William Pitt the elder. George survived a Jacobite rebellion and was the last King to lead his troops in battle. During his reign, his son, William Duke of Cumberland (commonly known as "The Butcher"), led his troops in the bloody Battle of Culloden Moor, which caused Bonnie Prince Charlie to flee to the Isle of Skye. George II, like his father, chased after the women. He was also the patron of Handel. He died of a heart attack at Westminster Palace in 1760.

1760 With George III, England again had to suffer another crazy George, this one nicknamed "Farmer George." One of the most outstanding events in the English history during George III's reign was the loss of America and the historic Boston Tea Party. Also during this period, the famous Battle of Trafalgar was won by our Lord Nelson, as was another famous battle in 1815, the Battle of Waterloo.

In 1765 King George III suffered his first bouts of madness. After treatment he seemed to revive and gained the favour of the people. However, he spent his last years in Windsor

Castle wandering around the basement corridors, talking to himself, with his hair hanging down to his waist. He eventually went blind and deaf and is reputed to have died of senility on January 29, 1820.

1820 George IV... If you thought George I was a bad King, this chap was even "wors-er-er." He was a fat, lazy drunkard, who spent much of his time gambling and got so deep into debt that Parliament stepped in and offered him a deal that he couldn't refuse. They told him that if he would marry Caroline of Brunswick they would pay his debt. (What they meant was the taxpayers would have to pay for this lay-about King.) He eventually died of internal bleeding and liver damage. (Now, I wonder how on earth he got that problem?)

1830 William IV was sixty-five years old when he inherited the crown. One of the major events that occurred during his reign was the abolition of slavery throughout the British Empire. William reluctantly helped to push the Reform Act, which was designed to shift the power from the sovereign and the aristocracy to the people. He was just like the other Georges in being accused of womanizing. He eventually died of liver failure and pneumonia.

1837 Queen Victoria... The most famous historical fact about Victoria's reign is that she holds the record as the longest-reigning monarch of England — over sixty-three years. During this long reign Great Britain ruled approximately one-quarter of the world. The saying at the time was that "the sun never set on British soil."

On the February 10, 1840 Victoria married a German (why-oh-why always Germans?), Prince Albert of Saxe-Coburg-Gotha. He seemed to be a great chap but died without notice while living at Windsor Castle. Victoria was Queen of the United Kingdom of Great Britain and Ireland and Empress of India, as well as twenty-eight major colonies in Africa and Asia from New Zealand to the Transvaal. Although Empress of India, she never set foot in the country, but during the Victorian period India's trade and industry made Great Britain the world's richest nation. People in other countries wanted products made in Great Britain.

WINDSOR

1901 Edward VII was the eldest son of Victoria's nine children. His nicknames were "The Peacemaker" and "Tum-Tum." (Please don't ask me why.) He was fifty-nine years of age when he became King. During his days as the Prince of Wales, Queen

Victoria disapproved of his free-and-easy life style which, during that period, caused quite a scandal for the monarchy. So the Queen tried to keep him out of the public eye. Here was another Prince of Wales who was a womanizer. He was known to have had at least thirteen mistresses. He also loved gambling, horse-racing, shooting, the theatre, yachting and travelling all over Europe. (At the time he had nothing else to do.) When he became King, he set out to strengthen relations between the French and the Russians but had problems with his nephew, Kaiser Wilhelm II of Germany. Edward died of bronchitis at Buckingham Palace on May 6, 1910.

1910 George V was known as the "Sailor King." He spent much of his time in the Royal Navy and worked his way up to vice-admiral. He was also Prince of Wales and created the position of Duke of York. When World War I with Germany broke out, George visited the western front regularly. After this war he was the monarch who changed his name because of the friction between the people of England and their King's "German relations." The family's original name was "Saxe-Coburg-Gotha," so they took the name of the favourite royal residence, Windsor Castle. Instead of collecting women, like the Georges before him, this George collected postage stamps. He had a world famous collection. George V died on January 20, 1936, of bronchitis at Sandringham House, Norfolk.

1936 Edward VIII was known as "Our Smiling Prince." He was an uncrowned King of England for only 325 days. On December 10, 1936, Edward shocked the country and the world by abdicating the throne in order to marry an American divorcee, Mrs. Wallis Warefield Simpson. (I can't see what was wrong with that. At least she wasn't another German!) After Edward married he lived in France, unreconciled with the royal family. He wanted to play a part in the Second World War, but, instead, was given the position of Governor of the Bahamas. He died of cancer on May 28, 1972 in Paris.

1936 George VI made a career in the Royal Navy and served during the First World War. Becoming King of England was, to him, very unexpected. He was a bit embarrassed by his stammer, but during his Navy career he virtually cured himself. In his early days of giving speeches, he still had a slight stammer, which, in time, he overcame.

During the Second World War he visited his troops in France and North Africa. His Christmas broadcast to the nation was a great success. His own residence, Buckingham Palace, was, in fact, bombed nine times during the war. He and his wife, Queen Elizabeth, were truly loved by the people of England. The people were saddened by the death of King George VI, on February 6, 1952 at Sandringham House, Norfolk. George had had an operation for lung cancer but died soon after.

1952 Queen Elizabeth II is Queen of the United Kingdom of Great Britain and Northern Ireland and other realms and territories, Head of the Commonwealth, and Head of State of fourteen of its members. She married Prince Philip, the Duke of Edinburgh, the only son of Prince Andrew of Greece. She was in Africa when told of the death of her father and that she now was Queen of England. Elizabeth made Philip a Prince of the United Kingdom and gave birth to Prince Charles on November 14, 1948.

Charles captured the attention of the world with his great royal wedding to Princess Diana. I think we all know what happened next. He got the two heirs to the throne, which was his main task of marrying a virgin bride. Meanwhile, waiting in the wings was his true love. So Charles dumped Diana and thought that things would soon calm down and that when they did he would introduce

Camilla (the one waiting in the wings.) Then he would settle down with her and that would be that. But Diana wouldn't go away. She was the great love of the people and the royals didn't like it one bit. She had to be eliminated. The rest, like all the other stories of the monarchs, is "history."

The Kings and Queens of England

The reason I have included the relevant dates of the Kings and Queens, is that many people find that a King or Queen was actually born, died, or was crowned on their birthday. Some people seem to adopt that monarch as their favorite and have studied them more in depth. Hopefully you will see your birth date in here somewhere.

Most historians start with William I, as he was crowned King of all England. There were claims that other Kings controlled all England, but history is a bit sketchy. The reason I have started with Edward the Confessor is that I find his memorial, Westminster Abbey, a treasure. He was succeeded by Harold. (How can you rule a kingdom with a name like Harold?) As you will see, Harold didn't last long. (I told you... it's all in the name).

KING (EADWEARN) EDWARD (Known as The Confessor)

Born in Islip, Oxfordshire 1003, crowned at Winchester 3 April 1042. Reigned for 23 years 294 days, died 5 January 1066. He was canonized in 1161. Unfortunately, he had no children. So, in compliance with the Witan Council, his cousin Harold was named to succeed him. Westminster Abbey was founded by King Edward, this is where his body is entombed.

KING HAROLD

Born in 1020. Crowned at Westminster Abbey 6 January 1066, reigned for a total of 283 days. He died after getting an arrow in his eye at Senlac Hill during the Battle of Hastings on 14 October 1066.

WILLIAM I (Known as the Conqueror)

Born in 1027. Started his reign 14 October 1066, he reigned for 20 years, 10 months and 26 days. William I died 9 September 1087, when his horse reared up violently, whilst stepping on hot ashes, causing the pommel of the saddle to rip into his stomach, causing great pain. He was 60. He is buried at St. Stephen's Abbey in Caen, Normandy. William I had nine children — three legitimate, named Robert, Henry and William.

WILLIAM II (Known as Rufus, which means red — his hair and complexion were the same color.)

Born in 1056. He succeeded the throne 10 September 1087, was crowned 26 September 1087 at Westminster Abbey. Reigned 12 years, 10 months and 24 days. He never married and had no children. He was also known as the "Blasphemous King." The historians recorded his death: "Whilst the King was hunting in the New Forest an arrow was fired and slighted off a wooden tree and hit the King a mortal blow." It's interesting to note that his brother, Henry, was in the woods hunting with him. As soon as Henry was informed of his brother's death, he put spurs to his horse and rushed to claim the treasures and crown at Winchester — which at that time, was the capital of England. William II is buried at Winchester Cathedral.

HENRY I (Known as the Lion of Justice)

Born in 1068. Started his reign 2 August 1100, crowned 5 August 1100 at Westminster Abbey. He reigned for 35 years, 3 months and 28 days. Died 1 December 1122 at the age of 67. His death was due to eating too many Lampreys (funny looking eel-type fish, which he loved). This triggered a surfeit and he consequently died.

A good King for England. He introduced the Judicial system, and abolished the "Cruel Tax Law" which had been established by William II.

STEPHEN

Born in 1097. Succeeded the throne 22 December 1135. Reigned 18 years, 10 months and 24 days. He died of a heart attack at St. Martin's Priory in Dover, 25 October 1154. Buried at Faversham Abbey in Kent. He had five children.

Stephen usurped the throne and put England into instant civil war. The monks, who were the recorders of history at this time, referred to Stephen's reign as: "the nineteen long winters, when God and his angels slept."

MATILDA (Known as Empress Maud)

Born February 1102. Succeeded the throne April 1141. Reigned for only seven months and three days. She died 10 September 1167 while in France. The cause of her death is obscure.

There was a time when she tricked her enemies into thinking she was dead. In 1141 she found herself trapped in the town of Devizes, Wiltshire by her enemies — Stephen's bad lot of men. She was locked up and told that she would never leave there alive. Her guards were told that Matilda was very ill and that she needed care. Stephen's lot refused her any help. Then her guards told the enemy that she would die if she didn't get help. Again she was denied help. Eventually, the enemy was told that she was dead and Stephen's lot celebrated while her attendants mourned her. Matilda's guards asked if they could take her body to Gloucester for burial. The enemy agreed saying "we don't want this stinking body in here." The corpse was tied to a stretcher and carried off to Gloucester. When Matilda's attendants were clear of Wiltshire they took the straps off of her body and up she got to the roaring laughter of her attendants. What a good job her enemies didn't agree to bury her right there. Smart lady!

HENRY II (Known as Curtmantel because of a short cloak he wore.)

Born 5 March 1133. Succeeded the throne 25 October 1154, crowned in Westminster Abbey on 19 December 1154. Reigned for 34 years, 8 months and 11 days. He died in France, at the age of 55, of blood poisoning from a wound on his heel. He was one of the great Henrys, but marred his career by allowing the slaughter of his once friend, Thomas-a-Becket (a name that rings down in English history). His wife ended up hating him and even turned his sons against him. He had 11 children — 3 illegitimate (no TV in those days)! There were five sons. The notable ones were: William, Henry, Richard and John. At Henry II's death the historians claimed he died a "Beaten Monarch."

RICHARD I (Known as Coeur de Lion, meaning Lionheart)

Born in Oxford, 8 September 1157. Succeeded to the throne 6 July 1189, crowned in Westminster Abbey, 3 September 1189. Reigned 9 years, 9 months and 12 days. Died on 6 April 1199, after being shot in the shoulder by a crossbow bolt. He is buried in France.

Many historians have painted a grand picture of Richard I, but with our modern technology use of carbon dating, we are proving the early historians wrong. For my money, Richard I was a pathetic excuse for a King. In a nut shell here's what he did: He sold land titles, buildings, castles, anything he could get his sticky fingers on to raise funds to go on the Crusades. He was quoted as saying, "I would sell London if I could find someone rich enough to buy it." Now, having drained most of the money from his country, he set off on a very long journey and met up with the other European would-be crusaders. This was the Third Crusade, to recapture the Holy Land of Palestine from those other chaps, the Muslims. It was reported that Richard I was a bloodthirsty, vicious and cruel man. For example, when he captured many prisoners in the "Siege at Acre" he slaughtered most of them himself, keeping some of them alive in case they ran out of food. Well, I've no need to say more.

He was King of England for roughly 10 years, and spent about 10 months actually in England. His wife, Berengaria of Navarre never set foot in England. They married in Limassol, Cyprus in 1191. He was captured on his way home from the Crusades in Austria by Emperor Henry VI, and held for a ransom of 150,000 marks. The money was raised by — guess who? — the taxpayers. When Richard I died he left the country *bankrupt*. What do you think of a King who does that to his country? Next time you see the movie "Robin Hood," with the welcoming home of King Richard I, you may wonder... did the people of England really greet this stranger King, who drained the country of its finances, in Hollywood fashion? They should let me write the script!

JOHN (Known as Bad King John)

Born in Oxford, 24 December 1116. Succeeded the throne 6 April 1199. Reigned 17 years, 6 months and 13 days. He died of dysentery at Newark Castle, 18 October 1216 and was buried at Worcester Cathedral.

When King John took the "gold hat," he also took a country that was penniless because of this Richard chap, the previous King. If you study the facts on John you will find that the Barons didn't like him, because he increased the taxes to raise revenue. The monks were against him for not getting an army together and go on this ridiculous crusading stuff.

(Remember, the monks recorded the history, so it's obvious that if they didn't like you, they're not going to write good stuff about you!) The Pope, Innocent III, was also against him because the Barons complained about him. Also, the King of France, King Philip Augustus, was out to get John. (That's not surprising the French were always against, well just about everyone!) The people of England were also against him because John put up the taxes in a time when the country was broke. So, with all these factors against him, he didn't have a good start, and it never seemed to get any better. Look at the Magna Carta. When you really study this Charter you will see that the main items are for the Barons' benefits... They wanted to secure their wealth and no King was going to take that away! (History repeats itself again.) The rich and famous people in power want to hold onto what they've got, and will go to all measures to keep it, even if it means dragging their King down. So, if you take another look at King John, you will find that he wasn't a bad King after all.

HENRY III

Born in Winchester on 1 October 1207. Succeeded the throne 18 October 1216, at the age of 9. Temporarily crowned in Gloucester Cathedral on 28 October 1216. On 17 May 1220 he declared himself of age to be officially crowned at Westminster Abbey. He reigned for 56 years and 29 days and died on 16 November 1272, at the age of 65. He is buried at Westminster Abbey. Henry III wasn't credited for being a very good King. In fact, his incompetence in ruling is what created Parliament. This is yet another case of a boy King who was dominated by his advisors. He did rebuild Westminster Abbey, and most of the cathedrals had a touch of Henry added to them over the years. Salisbury Cathedral was also built during his reign. So, to sum this chap up, he was ambitious, arrogant, impractical, and a coward.

EDWARD I (Known as Longshanks, which means "long legs." Also known as "The Hammer of the Scots")

Born in Westminster Palace 17 June 1239. Succeeded the throne on 20 November 1272, crowned in Westminster Abbey 18 August 1274. He reigned for 34 years, 7 months and 21 days. He died on the Scottish border of a severe stroke affecting his face and left side. He's buried at Westminster Abbey.

Edward I was a great statesman and a military genius. He was very worthy of the title "King of England." One of the first things he did was to sort out Wales. He took control of the whole area and made his first born son the Prince of Wales. In every monarchy since Edward I, the eldest son born automatically becomes the Prince of Wales. Edward's next ambition was to conquer Scotland, which sadly, he never did. What a great pity that future Kings were not molded like this great chap.

EDWARD II (Known as Caernarfon)

Born in Caernarfon Castle, Wales 25 April 1284. Succeeded to the throne on 7 February 1307, crowned in Westminster Abbey 25 February 1308. Reigned for 19 years, 6 months and 13 days. Abdicated on 20 January 1327, at Kenilworth Castle, Warwickshire. Murdered at Berkeley Castle, Gloucester, 21

September 1327. Edward II is on the list as being one of the worst Kings that ever sat on the English throne. Some historians even suspect that he was not Edward I's son — that he was switched or smuggled into the birthing room. He was nothing like his great father... he was a completely different breed. He was homosexual and took a lover called Piers Gaveston to whom he was addicted. He totally ignored the nobility — he just went through the motions of running his affairs. The Barons were sick as a parrot about this. They lured Piers Gaveston out of Warwick Castle and hacked his head off! Edward II rebelled and lured another fancy man into his court. Then his attitude got worse. So, this weak King was deposed and put in dungeons where the guards had their way with him and mocked him continuously. He suffered the worst death of all Kings.

EDWARD III (Known as Caernarfon)

Born in Windsor Castle 13 November 1312. Succeeded the throne 25 January 1327. Crowned in Westminster Abbey 29 January 1327. Reigned for 50 years, 4 months and 27 days. Died 21 June 1377 and was buried at Westminster Abbey.

Edward was considered to be an affable and majestic King. A tremendous military commander who, when in battle, would shout: "Come on!" rather than "Go on!" He started the hundred year war. (How did he know it would go on for a 100 years?) One of his 12 sons was known as the Black Prince, who certainly left his name in history. The Black Prince's face was scarred by arrows from wars he had fought at the age of 15. Sadly, he died without notice in 1376.

Edward also founded the Order of the Garter, which was similar to the Knights of the Round Table. There was also a sad ending for this great King who suffered all sorts of setbacks, like the Black Plague (Bubonic Plague) which wiped out over 800,000 of his people. All that he won in France was lost because he didn't have the army to defend it. He eventually died of a stroke and while dying, before his body was even cold, his faithless mistress stole the rings off his fingers and his staff stripped him of his belongings and left him lying naked on the floor.

RICHARD II (Known as Richard of Bordeaux)

Born in Bordeaux, France on 6 January 1367. Succeeded the throne 22 June 1367. Crowned at Westminster Abbey 16 July 1377. Reigned 22 years, 3 months and 8 days. Abdicated 29 September 1399 (in the Tower of London). Murdered in Pontefract Castle, 14 February 1400. Buried at Kings Langley Hertfordshire, then reburied at Westminster Abbey in 1413. Another useless King, he started off alright but then slipped into decline. He is said to have introduced the handkerchief. (My question is, what did they use before?) He also terminated the war with France by marrying the French King's daughter when she was only seven years old. There is a royal painting of him hanging in Westminster Abbey, on the right hand side as you go in.

HENRY IV (Known as, well... Henry IV)

Born at Bolingbroke Castle, Lincoln in 1367. Succeeded the throne 30th September 1399, crowned in Westminster Abbey 13 October 1399. He reigned for 13 years, 5 months and 13 days and died on 20 March 1413 at the age of 46, in the Jerusalem Chambers Westminster Palace. Buried at Canterbury Cathedral.

Shakespeare described Henry's reign as "A scrambling and unquiet time." During his reign, between 1399 and 1410, there was nothing but rebellion after rebellion. At the close of Henry's reign he became very sick. He was no doubt suffering from leprosy and was seen wandering around the Jerusalem Chambers. You see, all of his life he wanted to go on the Crusades, like some of the Kings before him. The Jerusalem Chambers was the nearest he would ever get. All he could do was dream, and he finally died in that very chamber.

HENRY V (Known as Henry of Monmouth

Born 16 August 1387. Succeeded the throne 20 March 1413. Crowned 9 April 1413 in Westminster Abbey, he reigned for only 9 years, 5 months and 11 days. Henry V died August 31 1422, at age 35. He is buried at Westminster Abbey in the Chapel of the Confessor.

This great King of England turned the country around and made it the strongest nation in the whole of Europe. Henry V was recognized as the heir of France when he had a tremendous victory in reviving the Hundred Year War with France. He won the famous Battle of Agincourt (1415), then took Normandy (1417), and took Paris in 1419. Henry didn't live long enough to wear the "gold hat" as King of France. Sadly, he died without notice. By the way, Henry V won his victories with the famous long bow. You see, it requires two fingers to pull the string back. These two fingers — without a bow — were used in jest to insult the French. Churchill reversed the fingers to give us the Victory sign.

HENRY VI

Born in Windsor Castle on 6 December 1421. Succeeded the throne 1 September 1422. Crowned in Westminster Abbey 6 November 1429 and 16 December 1431 at St. Denis, Paris then St. Paul's Cathedral 13 October 1470. (There's nothing like making sure that the people know who is King.) He reigned for 38 years, 6 months and 4 days. He was deposed on the 4 March 1461, and restored as monarch on 3 October 1470. He was again deposed 11th April 1471 and died, well... he was murdered on 21 May 1471, at the Tower of London. Henry VI is buried at Cheeriest Abbey and Windsor Castle and at Westminster Abbey. No, please don't ask. Here is a King of all England and King of France at the age of only nine months he was the first royal to wear a nappie, (known to some as a diaper).

Henry VI was, in one word, a "tragic" King. England had gained quite a large area of France and slowly, all that was gained was lost. Joan of Arc rebelled and called the English the "Goddams." She was captured in 1428 and sold to the British. She was promptly burned at the stake and her ashes were thrown in the river. About 20 years after her execution she was retried by the Pope Calixtus III, found not guilty and promptly made into a saint.

EDWARD IV

Born in Rouen, France 28 April 1442. Succeeded the throne 4 March 1461 and again 11th April 1471. Crowned 28 June 1461 in

Westminster Abbey. Reigned for 22 years and 36 days. Died 9 April 1483 at Westminster Palace, at the age of 40.

I suppose he was not a bad King in some respects, but he sold out to the French in 1475 when King Louis XI paid Edward 75,000 crowns and promised an annual sum of 20,000 if he would return to England and leave France alone. Edward did so, and did very nicely out of the deal. A year later, in 1476, William Caxton returned to England (maybe they paid him off as well). During Edward's reign the famous War of the Roses took place — a long story, which I won't go into now. The last great battle was at Towton (No, not toytown) where the Yorks beat the Lancastrians. This is where the famous Earl of Warwick, the "Kingmaker," was brutally killed. The King suddenly died without notice and he left the kingdom to his son, Prince Edward — another boy King until his uncle came up with an idea...

EDWARD V

Born in Westminster at the Abbot's House on 2 November 1470. Succeeded the throne 9 April 1483, but not crowned. He reigned for only 3 months, 16 days. Deposed 25 June 1483.

Edward's wicked uncle Richard booked a room at the Tower of London for Edward and his nine-year-old brother. He had them safely locked away under his full control. It was hardly a place where they could send a postcard to their mum. Their wicked uncle Richard was after one thing: the crown of England. He destroyed anyone that stood in his way, or were related, paving the way to his goal. As for the two princes, they conveniently disappeared. Richard just threw up his hands when challenged as to the princes' whereabouts (just like Vana White when someone gets a letter wrong.) Their bodies were found hidden beneath the stairs in the "Bloody Tower" some 400 years later.

RICHARD III, Usurper (Known as Richard Crookback and "Old Dick")

Born at Fortheringhay Castle, Northamptonshire 2 October 1452. Succeeded the throne on 26 June 1483. Crowned at Westminster Abbey 6 July 1483. Reigned for only two years, two months. He was killed at the battle of Bosworth, Leicestershire on 22 August 1485, at age 42.

During the Battle of Bosworth his body was badly mutilated, stripped naked, thrown on the back of a horse and cart and taken to the nearby Greyfriar's Church, Leicester where he was buried in an unmarked grave. Later his remains were dug up and thrown into the river and his stone coffin was used as a drinking trough for animals on a farm.

Now... at this famous Battle of Bosworth, a chap by the name of Henry found the King's crown in a thorn bush, stuck it on his head, and here another King Henry emerged to rule the country. (Incidentally... Richard III was known as the last of the Medieval Kings of England.)

HENRY VII (Known as Henry VIII's Dad)

Born Pembroke Castle, South Wales 28 January 1457. Succeeded the throne on 22 August 1485. Crowned in Westminster Abbey 30th October 1485. Reigned for 23 years 8 months. Died on 23 April 1509, at age 52. Buried in Westminster

Abbey. Henry VII was the first of the Tudor Kings. Just like many Kings before him, he eliminated any person that had even the slightest claim to the throne. He established the country and, in fact, brought his own and the country's economy to an all time high. He was severely shocked at his son's death. Prince Arthur, the Prince of Wales, was to have been the heir to the throne. He died without notice, which paved the way for Henry VII's next son, the famous Henry VIII, to take the crown.

Henry VIII (Known as Bluff King Hal)

Born at Greenwich Palace, Kent 28 June 1491. Succeeded the throne on 22nd April1509. Crowned in Westminster Abbey 24 June 1509. Reigned for 37 years, 9 months and 6 days. Died 28 January 1547 at age 56. He was buried in St, George's Chapel, Windsor Castle.

Well... this is a King that is well known to most people. If you ask someone to name a King of England, the chances are it will be King Henry VIII. He is mainly remembered for introducing "wife disposal." As you know, he had six wives — which is not so uncommon in today's world. The dissolution of monasteries in 1536 was another major reason he is remembered. He closed down 823 Monasteries and had them destroyed beyond repair. He then became head of the Church of England and added more ships to his now great Navy. What must be remembered about Henry VIII's reign is that he was loved by the people. He did not demand heavy taxes as did previous Kings. This is one of the greatest qualities of a King — to have the people behind him. He certainly had that.

EDWARD VI

Born in Hampton Court Palace, 12 October 1537, son of Henry VIII's third wife, Jane Seymour. Succeeded the throne on 28 January 1547 at the age of nine. He was crowned 19 February 1547 in Westminster Abbey and died 6 July 1553, at Greenwich Palace at the age of 16. He is buried at Westminster Abbey in the Henry VII Chapel.

Now, here was another chap who was under the guidance of his Uncle — Edward Seymour, the Duke of Somerset. Edward was a sickly lad and there was a constant power struggle amongst his nobles. The nobles knew Edward VI wouldn't live long, so they were very concerned as to who would wear the "gold hat" next. Edward struck out any chance of his half-sisters, Mary and Elizabeth, succeeding him, by appointing Lady Jane Grey. By this time there was great friction between the Protestants and the Catholics. Lady Jane was used in a plot to usurp the throne. She was the daughter of the Duke of Northumberland. The Duke was pushing his family into this powerful position and persuaded young Edward to approve the deal. The King was hated by most nobles for appointing Lady Jane Grey. Do you think they were going to let him get away with this? King Edward VI died of consumption. (I strongly believe that the King was killed by poison for having made this decision... who knows?)

LADY JANE GREY

Born 15 September 1537, proclaimed Queen 10 July 1553. (Although she was claimed Queen, she was never crowned.) She only lasted 9 days.

This 17-year-old young lady was sent to the tower with her young husband. She watched as they took her husband to have his head removed and saw his headless body being brought back. Then, it was her turn... she had practiced in her cell the laying down of her head, but when it came time to do it she was blindfolded. She reached out with her hands saying: "Where is it... what do I do? I don't know what to do!" No one did anything, until the axeman gently laid her head on the block. On 12 February 1554 Lady Jane was beheaded. Her Uncle Northumberland, who put her in this position, was also executed for the same crime: treason. Then the Lord Mayor of London proclaimed Edward's sister, Mary, to be the rightful Queen of England. Once again, history took another turn. Lady Jane Grey is buried at the Tower of London. Look for her in the chapel, called St. Peter ad Vincula. Also in the Chapel you can see a list of other people who were executed in the Tower.

MARY I (Known as Bloody Mary, the famous drink is also attributed to her name.)

Born at Greenwich Palace 8 February 1516, proclaimed Queen on 19 July 1553 and crowned 1 October 1553 in Westminster Abbey. Mary I reigned for 5 years, 4 months and 11 days. She died 17 November 1558 at St James' Palace, London. She is buried in Westminster Abbey.

This woman was a devout Roman Catholic who married Prince Philip II of Spain in Winchester Cathedral 25 July 1554. (With this Spanish connection, it's a wonder that we didn't end up with our Fish & Chips wrapped up in tortillas!) Her main goal was to rid the country of Protestants, and secure Catholicism as the religion of the nation. She did this by burning anyone who wouldn't convert to Catholicism. Two-hundred-eighty-three people perished this way and the famous Archbishop Crammer was tortured and forced to sign his conversion of the faith. To this Mary said: "I will save his soul... burn him!" This was done at Oxford.

Mary joined with Spain in a war on France and lost Calais, France. (If you have ever seen Calais then you know we didn't lose much.) She died of influenza at Lambeth Palace at the young age of 42. In the room where Mary died a prayer book was found, opened and stained with tears. She was no doubt crying because she had no children to succeed her. I expect there were teeth marks on her bed posts, knowing that her protestant sister Elizabeth was to succeed her. Here, again, history took a dramatic turn.

ELIZABETH I (Known as "Good Queen Bess" and "The Virgin Queen Gloriana")

Born at Greenwich Palace on 7 September 1533, Elizabeth succeeded to the throne on 17 November 1558. She was crowned on 15 January 1559 in Westminster Abbey and reigned for 44 years, 4 months and 7 days. She died at Richmond Palace 24 March 1603 at the age of 70 and was buried in Westminster Abbey.

The fist thing Elizabeth did was to stabilize the country with her Protestant religion. Incidently, most people stayed with the Protestant religion even when all the burning was going on.

Little did Mary know, that her actions did more to drive people away from Catholicism. During the reign of Elizabeth I, England had one of the greatest monarchs to ever sit on the English throne. She was very cautious and demanding, yet very popular with the people. She stabilized the nation, and England became one of the wealthiest countries in the world. When Elizabeth knew she was dying she would not go to bed, but instead, laid around on pillows and cushions trying not to drop off to sleep for fear that if she did she would not wake up. Eventually she died of blood poisoning caused by a tonsillar abscess.

JAMES I, also **JAMES VI of Scotland** (Known as "The Wisest Fool in Christendom.")

Born in Edinburgh Castle, 19 June 1566. Succeeded the throne on 24 July 1567, in Scotland, and 24 March 1603 in England. Reigned for 22 years and 3 days in England. In Scotland, 57 years and 46 days.

James I was the son of Mary Queen of Scots. He was another King who thought that he had the divine right, and was answerable only to God. He escaped the blowing up of Parliament on 5 November 1605 — all his reign was recorded as "troubled." In 1611 he gave the thumbs-up for the authorized version of the Bible, which has since become known as the "King James Version." What made people sick as a parrot was that he also gave the thumbs-up for the execution of Sir Walter Raleigh, on a charge of fighting the Spanish 13 years previously. This was done to keep the peace with Spain. James died on 27 March 1625 of kidney failure.

CHARLES I

Born in Dunfermline Palace, Scotland on 19 November 1600, Charles I succeeded the throne on 27 March 1625. He was crowned 2 February 1626 in Westminster Abbey and reigned for 23 years, 10 months and 3 days. He died 30 January 1649 in Whitehall London, at the age of 48. He was the only King of England to lose his head.

Charles I, like his father, tried to rule England by divine right — answerable only to God and ignoring Parliament. In fact, he dissolved Parliament three times and ruled the country without them from 1629-1640. He married Henrietta Maria, the sister of King Louis XIII of France. The problem was, she was a staunch Catholic while Charles I and England were Protestant. Her main goal was to convert the King and, in turn, the country. Friction built between them on this matter.

Parliament got sick as a parrot over the King demanding money for his worthless wars. Eventually things went from bad to worse and when he tried to seize five dissident members of Parliament for treason a civil war was sparked, which started with the Battle of Edge Hill, on 23 October 1642. The King was eventually put on trial for treason, found guilty, and beheaded in Whitehall, London. (The building opposite the Horse Guards Parade.) As you will notice, the date he was beheaded was in January and it was bitter cold, so Charles I wore two shirts in case he shivered with the cold, making the people think that he was nervous.

OLIVER CROMWELL (Known as Lord Protector)

Born in Huntingdon 1599, he took over as Protector on 11 December 1653. He died on 3 September 1659 of a fever and is buried in Westminster Abbey. After The Restoration, his remains were dug up and taken to the tyburn. There he was hung, drawn and quartered. (He never uttered a word!) What was left was thrown into the river Thames.

Cromwell was a great soldier and statesman, but marred his career when he allowed the massacres in Ireland. (A great film to watch is "Cromwell," starring Richard Harris and Alex Guinness... this explains the whole story of Charles I and Cromwell.)

CHARLES II (Known as the "Merry Monarch")

Born in St. James Palace, 29 May 1630. Succeeded the throne 30th January 1649. Restored the monarchy 29 March 1660. He was crowned 23 April 1661 in Westminster Abbey. Charles II reigned 36 years and 7 days and died in Whitehall Palace 6 February 1685. He is buried in Westminster Palace in the Henry VII Chapel.

Although he was married to Catherine of Braganza, he only produced one legitimate son — James, Duke of Monmouth. He did manage to produce 13 illegitimate children, however. Charles was a very weak King. It was said of him that "He never said a foolish thing and never did a wise one." While in exile in France, he was always short of money. On one occasion he was so desperate for money that he actually *sold* Dunkirk back to France for 400,000 English pounds!

During his reign the Great Plague of London was followed by the Great Fire of London in 1666. At this time a two party system in Parliament came into being — the Whigs and Tories. Toward the end of Charles' reign he began going downhill, losing his powers.

Shortly after changing his religion to Catholicism, at the age of 55, he died of uremia and mercury poisoning.

JAMES II (Known as James VII of Scotland)

Born in St. James Palace, London 14 October 1633. Succeeded the throne 6 February 1685. Crowned 23 April 1685 in Westminster Palace. He reigned for only three years, nine months and seven days. James II died at age 68 on 6 September 1701. He is buried at Chateau of Saint Germain-en-Laye, near Versailles Paris.

Here England suffered another King who had no idea how to be a King. Most of his enemies were sick as a parrot over the way James was ruling the country, so they sent for the Protestant, William II of Orange, to come over and bring with him a large force to take the crown. Well, James took one look and popped over to France to hide. Parliament declared on 12 February 1689 that James had abdicated. William III and Mary II accepted the throne when it was offered. James returned with an army, via Ireland, but was defeated by William. Back to France, James went, where he was never to see England again.

WILLIAM III (known as King Billy)

William was born in Holland, 4 November 1650 and was proclaimed King 13 February 1689. He was crowned 11 April 1689 in (where else?) Westminster Abbey. William III reigned for 13 years, 23 days and died 8 March 1702, at age 52, in Kensington Palace.

One of William's actions that blotted his reign, was that he allowed the Massacre of Glencoe in the Highlands of Scotland. William III died from his wounds, which were incurred when his horse stumbled on a mole hill. This is why the Scots drink a "Jacobite Toast" to the little gentleman in the velvet jacket... meaning the little mole.

MARY II

Born St. James' Palace 30 April 1662. Proclaimed Queen 13 February 1689. Crowned 11 April 1689 in Westminster Abbey. Mary II reigned for 4 years, 10 months and 5 days. She died in Kensington Palace, 28 December 1694, of smallpox at the young age of 32. She is buried in Westminster Abbey.

ANNE

Born in St. James' Palace 6 February 1665. Succeeded the throne on 8 March 1702. Crowned 23 April 1702. Reigned for 12 years, 4 months and 24 days. Died on 1 August 1714 in Kensington Palace, she was 49. Buried in Westminster Abbey.

Anne was married to Prince George of Denmark. Charles II said of him, "I have tried him drunk and sober, and there is *nothing in him.*" She was so upset for having 17 children— and they all died. One of the important constitutional acts of her reign was when she sealed the Act of Union between England and Scotland in 1707 — hence the term, "Great Britain."

Anne weighed over 300 pounds and had difficulty moving around. When she finally died, the Doctor said: "Death was never more welcome than rest was to a weary traveler." Anne died of a stroke and was the last monarch of the Stuarts.

GEORGE I

Born in Osnabruck, Hanover 28 May 1660, George I succeeded the throne 1 August 1714, and was crowned 20 October 1714 in Westminster Abbey. He reigned for 12 years, 10 months and 10 days. He died on 11th June 1727 at age 67 and is buried in Hanover.

This was the start of the fat, non-English-speaking Germans who thought more of their own country than the country which elected them King. England had already suffered over 800 years of rulers from just about everywhere. We had the Celtics, Romans, Danish, Normans, French, Welsh, Scottish, Dutch and now the Germans. George I did not even try to speak English. When he came to England he brought with him two mistresses, leaving his wife, Sophia, locked up for life because he was suspicious that she had had an affair. He was quite content to let his favorite minister rule (now known as the Prime-Minister). The first chap was called Sir Robert Walpole. George I died on his way to Hanover where he spent most of his time. (For all the good he did, he might as well have stayed there in the first place.)

GEORGE II (Known as "Another German King")

Born in Herrenhausen, Hanover on the 30th October 1683. He succeeded the throne on 11 June 1727. Crowned on the 11 October 1727 in Westminster Abbey. He reigned for 33 years, 4 months and 14 days and died on 25 October 1760, at age 76. He is buried in the Henry VII Chapel, Westminster Abbey. (Did you know that King George II was the last King to be buried in Westminster Abbey?)

One of the notable historical events that he is remembered for was "Culloden Moor" in the Highlands of Scotland — a name that rings down in Scottish history. It was in 1745 that the Stuarts tried to restore the throne to Prince Charles Edward Stuart, grandson of James II, known as "The Young Pretender." Well, without going into too much detail, the King's second son, William Duke of Cumberland, became known as the "Butcher Cumberland" because of the tremendous massacre that took place. The flower "Sweet William" was named after the King's son and the town, Fort William, also bears his name. The Scots came up with a good name for William.. they called him "Stinking Billie" after a stinkwort waterweed.

As a foot note, George II died of a heart attack. He was also the last King of England to lead an army into battle. George II is buried in Windsor Castle.

GEORGE III (Known as "Farmer George")

Born in St. James Square, London 4 June 1738. Succeeded the throne 25 October 1760. Crowned 22 September 1761 in Westminster Abbey. Reigned for 59 years, 3 months and 3 days. Died in Windsor Castle 29 January 1820, age 81.

Well... we all know what George III is famous for: Losing America! If you think that the other two Georges were useless as Kings of England, well here was a total bafoon. When he became King he wanted to rule England just like the old medieval Kings had done. He wanted to go everywhere wearing his crown and do away with Parliament.

We all remember the Boston Tea Party in 1773, when colonists threw away 18,000 pounds (in monetary terms) of good tea, into the Boston harbor. (Do you realize how many nice cups of tea that would have made? Well, a lot!) George had an adviser that was getting all the blame, his name was "Lord Scotch Bute." Londoners hated him, so they lit a large bonfire in protest, where they burned lots of old boots — a pun on the name "Bute." They also burned petticoats to represent George's Mum. King George ended up completely mad, spending his last years wandering around the corridors of Windsor Castle, muttering to himself, wearing his favorite long purple dressing gown, with his beard nearly touching the floor. He must have looked a sight! He must have done something right, because he had nine sons and six daughters. (Well, no television in those days.)

GEORGE IV (Known by his nickname "Prinny")

Born in St. James Palace, 12 August 1762. Succeeded the throne 29 January 1820. Crowned 19 July 1821 in Westminster Abbey. Reigned for 10 years, 9 months and 15 days. George IV died in Windsor Castle on 26 June 1830, at age 67and is buried in Windsor Castle.

This chap, when he was Prince of Wales, had a string of mistresses, gambled, and became heavily in debt. He secretly married a Catholic widow named Maria Fitzerbert. The government said they would settle his debt if he would drop Maria and marry George's cousin, Caroline of Brunswick. He agreed, and when introduced to her he said, "Pray that I must be ill... fetch me a brandy!" They got married and he spent most of the evening "Drunk as a Lord," which is where this saying comes from. Well, he somehow consummated the marriage because his wife produced a girl, who died soon after birth. One thing that George's lazy lifestyle did, was to damage the monarchy's image. Lots of things happened during his reign. The Georgian and Regency styles were introduced. Also, he was a great admirer of Jane Austin. He kept a set of her novels at each palace. George IV died from internal bleeding and severe liver damage, due to consuming vast amounts of liquor.

WILLIAM IV (Commonly known as "Silly Billy")

Born in Buckingham Palace 21 August 1765, William IV succeeded the throne 26 June 1830. He was crowned 8 September 1831 in Westminster Abbey after a reign of 6 years, 10 months and 15 days. He died 20 June 1837, at age 71, of pneumonia and liver failure. He is buried in St. Georges Chapel, Windsor Castle. At last, a King who was born in England! He was nearly 65 when he took the throne. Here we had another King who didn't even want a Coronation Ceremony when he was crowned. He hated all this pomp and ceremony. He even used to offer people a lift in his carriage. Before he became King he was put in the Navy because Parliament didn't know what to do with him. He was pals with Horatio, Lord Nelson. When Nelson was shot by a sniper, William was given the bullet as a souvenir, which he apparently treasured. William was renowned for his womanizing, and managed to have 10 illegitimate children by his actress friend, Dorothea Jordan. He also had two legitimate daughters who died in infancy.

VICTORIA (Her nickname was "Grandmother of Europe")

Born in Kensington Palace 24 May 1812. Succeeded the throne 20 June 1838, crowned 28 June 1838. Victoria reigned for 63 Years, 10 months and 15 days. (She still holds the record for the longest reign of all the British monarchs.) She died in Osborne House, Isle of Wight on 22 January 1901. Victoria didn't want to be buried at Windsor Castle amongst her Hanoverian uncles. She was buried at Frogmore House, Windsor.

Her father died when she was only eight months old. She had a very strict upbringing by her mother and her Uncle Leopold of Saxe-Coburg. Victoria was very shy and never seemed to be invited to parties. She spent most of her time playing by herself. When she was told that she was Queen of England, she bawled her eyes out for a couple of days. When her governess got her under control this five-foot, pop-eyed, stout, future monarch — pulling herself together, said: "I'll be good."

She married another German, Prince Albert of Saxe-Coburg-Gotha on 10 February 1840. (Why another German?) Things were going well. They had four sons and five daughters, The royal family lived at Windsor Castle. Prince Albert loved to drink plenty of water each day. The problem was, the sewer system was backing up into the water, and this is what finally killed Prince Albert. Victoria never got over his death, for the rest of her life she wore black, and apparently was only seen to smile twice in public. There is so much to talk about Victoria, so I shall leave it here, with just a note: Did you know that Queen Victoria had Prince Albert's butler lay out his clothes on his bed, set a place at the dining room table for him each night and do everything as if he was still alive? She wouldn't let him go.

EDWARD VII (Known as the Peacemaker, and his nickname was Tum-Tum)

Born in Buckingham Palace, 9 November 1841, Edward succeeded to the throne on 22 January 1901. He was crowned 9 August 1902 in Westminster Abbey and reigned for nine years, six months and five days. He died in Buckingham Palace, 6 May 1910 at age 68 and is buried in St. Georges Chapel, Windsor Castle.

Edward became King after hanging around waiting for Queen Victoria to either retire, or... do *something*! He was another monarch who was a ladies' man. He was known to have had 13 mistresses. He also travelled just about everywhere before he became King. Well... he didn't have anything else to do... but it all came in handy, because when he became King he had accumulated many contacts in other countries and became known as "Edward the Peacemaker." He was also a great sportsman — he raced a yacht called "Britannia," and he was the only King to have won the Derby with a horse called "Minoru" in 1909. King Edward VII died of bronchitis.

GEORGE V (He was known as the Sailor King)

Born Marlborough House, London 3 June 1865, George V succeeded the throne 6 May 1910, crowned 22nd of June 1911 in

Westminster Abbey. Reigned for 25 years, 7 months and 6 days. Died of bronchitis at Sandringham House, Norfolk on 20 January 1936 at age 70. He is buried at St. George's Chapel, Windsor Castle.

George V was in the Navy for many years and rose to the rank of Vice Admiral. When Great Britain was at war with Germany, in World War I, the King regularly visited the western front and was a casualty of war himself. While in France he received serious injuries when his horse rolled on him.

Because of the German name, Saxe-Coburg-Gotha, the people of Britain were not happy with a King of German origin. So he decided to change the name of the royals and settled on the name: Windsor, after the castle where all the ancestors are buried. He was also the first monarch to broadcast to his subjects on Christmas Day (in 1932).

EDWARD VIII (Known as the "Smiling Prince")

Born in Richmond Park on 23 June 1894, succeeded the throne 20 January 1936, reigned uncrowned for 325 days, abdicated 10 December 1936 and died 28 May 1972 in Paris. Edward VIII is Buried at Frogmore House, Windsor Home Park.

As history records, the people of England were amazed that the the Prince of Wales would *abdicate* for the sake of a divorced American woman. (Well, let's face it, it was better than a German woman!) Sadly, the royal family threw him out — even out of the country. It was a tragic loss to England as he had the qualities of a fine King.

GEORGE VI

Born at York Cottage, Sandringham, Norfolk, 14 December 1895. Succeeded the throne on 11 December 1936. Crowned 12 May 1937 in Westminster Abbey. Reigned for 15 years. George VI died not long after an operation for lung cancer on 6 February 1952 in Sandringham House, Norfolk. He is buried at St. George's Chapel, Windsor Castle.

When King George was a Prince his title was Prince Albert. So why the change of names? Well... before Queen Victoria died, she decreed that no future monarch should bear her late husband's name, Albert. Respecting that request, the King changed his name.

George had a bit of a stammer which he mastered with great skill. He was also left-handed. This was not the done thing — for a King to have a defect — so when he was a lad he was forced to use his right hand by having his left hand tied behind his back.

ELIZABETH II

Born in 17 Bruton Street, London on 21 April 1926. Succeeded the throne 6 February 1952. Crowned on 2 June 1953. To date, still going strong. And the story and history of the Kings and Queens of England will continue... or will it?

Interpretations

"Died without notice"... If somebody has had a prolonged illness and isn't getting any better, there is always the thought that he or she could die. But if a person hasn't suffered a serious illness and has just dropped down dead, then he or she has "died without notice."

"Worse-er-er"... If things or people aren't getting any better, then they are getting worse. If they still don't get any better, then they are 'worse-er-er' than they were before... Do you understand? If not, lets get onto the next terms, because they get worse-er-er.

"Popped his clogs"... This is an old English expression. In the early days when somebody died, his most valuable item, his footwear, was automatically removed. Most people wore clogs in the early days, and these were a costly item. So, as soon as someone was pronounced dead (no doubt after he got worse-er-er) his clogs were removed and handed down in the family or donated to a close friend.

"Gold hat"... When I refer to someone wearing a gold hat, I am indicating a King or Queen. If you saw a crowd of people and someone asked which one was the King, you would simply say, "Oh, the chap with the gold hat on." This is a term that I frequently use in the tour business.

"Wednesday and it was raining"... I also use this term a lot in the tour business, because when talking about the history of England one is sometimes bombarded with all sorts of dates — even I can't remember them all. So, when I give a date I tell tourists that it was "Wednesday and it was raining." Then at least if they can't remember the date, they will remember what day it was and that it was raining.

About the Author

LESTER MORRIS says he was born at a very early age and is 100% British, with — maybe — just a dash of Viking. He spent sixteen early years in an orphanage. Most of his adult life he has been involved in the tour business and from this came his great love of English history.

On one of his three-week tours of England, Lester met his (now) wife, Valerie (from Austin, Texas). He moved to Texas in 1984 and after thirteen years is still trying to get used to the Mexican food. He says, "It's the only food I know of that reaches parts of the body no other food can get to!" After eating it he claims, "You have to place two toilet rolls in the refrigerator for the following morning."

Lester Morris runs his own business, ***The British Connection***. His company gives advice about travel in Great Britain and Lester himself conducts tours to the "Old Country." He also speaks to groups on various subjects having to do with Great Britian, including The Kings and Queens of England, Haunted England, Stonehenge, Crop Circles, The Tower of London and many, many more.

Lester is a member of *The South Texas Professional Speakers Association* and teaches cooking classes at Central Market in Austin on (what else?) how to cook **Good British Food**. He is currently working on a book entitled *The Green Penny-Farthing Bike,* about his life in an English orphanage.

To order additional copies of

"Did You Knows?"
of England

or for information about other books

by **Lester Morris** you

can contact him directly by email at

britconnct@aol.com

or by calling

1-800-725-0208